Philharmonic Concerto

PIERS BURTON-PAGE

Philharmonic Concerto

The Life and Music of Sir Malcolm Arnold

Methuen

First published in Great Britain in 1994
by Methuen London
an imprint of Reed Consumer Books Ltd
Michelin House, 81 Fulham Road, London SW3 6RB
and Auckland, Melbourne, Singapore and Toronto

A CIP catalogue record for this book
is available from the British Library
ISBN 0 413 45651 X

Printed and bound in Great Britain
by Mackays of Chatham plc

This book is dedicated with love

to my wife Maggie

Contents

List of Illustrations

All photographs from the composer's collection, with the exception of 6 – Mrs Betty Matthews; 7 – Royal College of Music; 17 – Mrs Annetta Hoffnung; 21 – Peter Okell; to all of whom grateful acknowledgement is extended. While every effort has been made to establish the copyright holders of the remaining photographs, it has not always been possible to do so; due acknowledgement will be made in future editions if further information is received.

Acknowledgements

Many people and institutions have helped me in the long process of gestation this book has undergone. Foremost among them is the composer himself, for over a long period Malcolm Arnold has allowed himself to be regularly bombarded with questions that must have seemed highly intrusive in nature. He has replied to them with uncommon patience and frankness, when severe irritation would have been much more in order. In recent years, as this book tells, he has been faithfully looked after by Anthony Day, to whom I owe an equal debt of gratitude, not least for his encouragement of this project when I sometimes felt daunted or that I had proceeded impossibly far down a blind alley.

Listing names is inevitably going to mean causing offence through sheer forgetfulness; but nevertheless the following have helped me in various ways and at various times and places, and I record my heartfelt thanks to them: John Amis; Martin Anderson; Jim Aspinall; Susan Bamert; Barbara Barker; Sally Cavender; John Gould; the late Sir Charles, and Lady Groves; Annetta Hoffnung; Georgina Ivor; Elsbeth Lindner; Betty Matthews; Donald Mitchell; Dorothy Morris; the late Archie Newman; Peter Okell; Michael Oliver; Christopher Palmer; Kriss Rusmanis; Lionel Salter; Fritz Spiegl; Ruth Tollington; Robert Matthew Walker. None of them can be held responsible for any facts, opinions or omissions that this book contains.

I also owe a considerable debt of gratitude to the following institutions, who have all responded to my persistent and sometimes off-beat enquiries with exemplary professionalism and forbearance: British Library; Faber Music; Royal College of Music; Alfred

Lengnick and Co.; National Sound Archive; Novello and Co.; and at the BBC: Central Reference Library; Music Library; Gramophone Library; Sound Archives. At my publisher, Methuen, Penelope Hoare and Rachel Peddie have both been towers of strength where support has been invaluable.

My largest debts of gratitude, however, are to my family; first to my father, John Burton-Page, for sustained encouragement, and for playing host to me during some periods of intense work on it; then to my mother, who knew of and supported my interest in this biography, and whose memory has sustained me in it; and then to my sons Andrew and Thomas for their continuing love, support and interest over the long period that they have had to live with this shadowy extra presence in the household. Lastly, the dedication at the front of this book expresses only a small fraction of the greatest debt I owe, one which I can never hope adequately to repay but for which my gratitude is boundless.

'For not infrequently there is no element of the *voluntary* in clowning. Often, d'you see, we take to clowning when all else fails. Under these impenetrable disguises of wet white, you might find, were you to look, the features of those who were once proud to be visible. You find there, per example, the *aérialiste* whose nerve has failed; the bare-back rider who took one tumble too many; the juggler whose hands shake so, from drink or sorrow, that he can no longer keep his balls in the air. And then what is left but the white mask of poor Pierrot, who invites the laughter that would otherwise come unbidden.

'The child's laughter is pure until he first laughs at a clown.'

Angela Carter, *Nights at the Circus*

Fanfare

for *An Individual Voice*

The picture usually held of the composer Malcolm Arnold is a distorted one. He is not another eccentric Englishman dabbling in his art without getting his feet wet, and his music is not all teeth and smiles. He is, on the contrary, a composer whose roots lie firmly in the European mainstream. His heroes include not only the great Viennese masters, Haydn, Mozart and Beethoven, but also Berlioz, Mahler and Sibelius. Not surprisingly, it is Malcolm Arnold's nine symphonies which are at the heart of his music-making: they present the whole man, warts and all, they express his deepest musical thoughts, and they demonstrate an aspect of the composer infinitely broader, more subtle and more complex than his popular image as the innocent-seeming author of breezy brass-band tunes, military marches, fanfares, comic capers for Gerard Hoffnung, pieces for children, toy symphonies, overtures for political occasions and those innumerable film scores. Yet these, too, are part and parcel of the composer, even if they are not the whole truth. There can seldom have been a musical life as richly diverse as that of Malcolm Arnold.

To see Malcolm Arnold whole is still difficult. For every Christmas television showing of the film *The Bridge on the River Kwai*, there are a hundred others with Arnold scores gathering dust on library shelves. Some of his music is still unpublished – the operas and ballets in particular. With one or two honourable exceptions, after a long period of neglect the record industry is now beginning to do him justice, both in his home country and abroad. We are beginning to grasp the scale of his achievement, the breadth of his musical range. There is the Arnold who can plumb the depths of tragedy in a Seventh Symphony of Mahlerian intensity; who has written two string quartets where beauty and ferocity movingly combine in intimate utterance; whose concertos, written out of love for his friends, such as Julian Bream, Richard Adeney, Yehudi Menuhin or Dennis Brain, uncannily meld the personality of their dedicatees with his own style and with the particular sonority of their instrument. Overshadowed perhaps by eminent contemporaries such as Benjamin Britten and Michael Tippett, and even Arnold's own close friend William Walton, this Malcolm Arnold still awaits proper exploration and true recognition.

So far, not much has been written about Arnold. Although Alan Poulton has compiled an admirable definitive catalogue of works and dates, the composer's life story, crammed with incident and involving encounters with many of the great names of music – and of Hollywood – has largely been a closed book. This first attempt can only hope to open some of the more colourful pages and is as much concerned with asking questions, or discussing the composer's ideas and preoccupations surrounding the music, and with relating his several musical worlds to each other as with offering even a tentative verdict. Hence the chapter headings, for instance, each of which unites the title of one of his more celebrated concert works with one of his many marvellous film scores. For this same reason I have regularly included Arnold's own comments on his music, as well as other topics, often expressed in his own pungent style. Quotations from him not otherwise attributed may be assumed to have been uttered by him in the course of our many encounters over the years.

As will be evident from the beginning, this book tries to relate Arnold's life to his music, and his music to his involvement in the everyday world. Therefore, the music itself is sometimes described – though not, I hope, in too technical a fashion, and with the minimum of jargon. Anyone seeking to go further into

Arnold's musical style and language is encouraged to consult Hugo Cole's admirable pioneering study, which contains a wealth of musical detail and analysis. The present book contains no music examples and there is no need to own a library of scores to follow the argument. Nor has it been my aim to be comprehensive in my coverage of the music, or to detail the background of every single piece the composer has written. Composers, after all, spend a great deal of time sitting at desks scratching their heads; not an activity that lends itself to continued reporting. Rather, it has been my aim to whet the appetite, and to encourage potential listeners to search out Arnold's splendid music on radio, records and tapes and in the concert hall. If more people are thereby persuaded to take Malcolm Arnold's music seriously, and to read, mark, learn and inwardly digest it for themselves, this book will have amply served its purpose.

It is all too easy when contemplating the life of an intensely creative human being to assume an inevitable connection between the life and the works. Particularly when the artist in question is still living, and there are family and friends with sensibilities of which it is only right to be mindful, perspectives will sometimes become distorted. Although Malcolm Arnold has only once or twice closed the door, this book cannot really be called the 'authorised biography' – that will have to wait. Rather it is Malcolm Arnold's life story largely told from his own standpoint. Even so, I am uncomfortably aware that it is the darker moments which stand out. Yet his many friends have testified that he has been to them the sunniest and most loyal of companions, full of kindness and compassion, humour and enthusiasm, consideration and courtesy. These are not the first qualities which spring to mind when writing about the symphonies, for instance. My title redresses the balance a little, however. It alludes not only to Thomas Russell's *Philharmonic Decade*, his inspiring history of the early days of the London Philharmonic Orchestra in which both he and Arnold played; it also refers to what I consider one of Malcolm Arnold's own most inspiriting pieces, written as a showpiece for that same orchestra. His *Philharmonic Concerto* is indeed a sunny work and never fails both to surprise and to entertain.

1 : A Grand Grand Overture

or *It Started in Paradise*

Malcolm Arnold's musical roots go back a long way. His father, William Arnold, traced them back[1] at least as far as Arnold's great-great-grandfather, William Hawes, who was born in 1785 and who was for over forty years a prominent figure in late Georgian and Regency London musical life. Hawes was a composer, mostly of small pieces for the gentlemen's catch-clubs of the period – one such glee, 'We're a-noddin'', sold 30,000 copies in two years. In his earlier years, William Hawes had been active as a singer at the Italian Opera House, and in 1801, at the age of sixteen, he was the youngest 'violin performer' in the Covent Garden Theatre Orchestra. Later he became a conductor, among whose achievements was the first English performance of Weber's *Der Freischütz*; and he was for twenty years Master of the Choristers and also Lutenist to King George III, holding important appointments at Westminster Abbey and St Paul's Cathedral. William Hawes died in 1846; the following year, his daughter Maria Hawes sang in the first-ever performance of *Elijah*, conducted by Mendelssohn himself in Birmingham Town Hall.

Malcolm Arnold's mother, Annie, was a descendant of William Hawes, and she inherited the family's strong musical instincts.

Arnold describes her as a very accomplished pianist and accompanist and she was to play an important part in his musical education. Her father had been a violinist and led a family string quartet, while his father in turn was for many years Chaplain of New College Oxford. On his retirement the Rev. Thomas Hawes accepted the living of Burgh Castle in Norfolk, where Arnold could recall occasional childhood visits; he remembered this Norfolk link when seeking a home nearer the end of his career.

On Arnold's father's side there was also evidence of musical leanings, even if they were less pronounced. William Arnold was a pianist and organist, in such time as was left to him from being Managing Director of Arnold Brothers, shoe-makers, the industry for which his native Northampton was famous. The Arnold family firm had been started by William Arnold senior, and the Arnold Bros factory, one of the principal ones in the city, stood in a prominent position near the centre of the town in St Giles's Terrace, a site now occupied by the headquarters of Barclaycard. Other scions of Northampton, much later occasionally to be cited with pride by Malcolm Arnold, were the sculptor Eric Gill and Edward Clark, a musician and senior musical administrator in the BBC, husband of the composer Elisabeth Lutyens.

Arnold's parents met through music, their lessons overlapping when they shared the same piano teacher in Northampton. Five children resulted from their eventual marriage, of whom Malcolm Henry Arnold, born on 21 October 1921, was the youngest. The family was a close one, cocooned in relative middle-class affluence thanks to the shoe-making business. Politics seems scarcely to have intruded, at least until the onset of the Depression at the end of the 1920s. As far as the youngest son was concerned, an early moment of political awakening seems to have come when his eldest brother Aubrey announced, to the dismay of his parents, that he was going to Spain to participate in the Spanish Civil War. He duly went, returning eventually to take over the family business. Aubrey's sense of honour was always strong. When, years later, the business collapsed under the twin pressures of recession and foreign competition, he took his own life. As the family grew up together in Northampton, Arnold was closest to his sister, Ruth, and to Philip, the brother immediately ahead of him. The two boys shared a room and played happily together as children. Not long after the outbreak of the Second World War, the still-young and recently-married Philip Arnold, who had joined the RAF, was shot down and killed in a raid over Berlin. The loss was a devastating blow not only to his brother – who had been writing pieces for Philip to play on the alto saxophone – but to the whole family and it bound Malcolm still closer to his mother, who throughout his formative years in Northampton had taken a protective interest in her unusually gifted son. He also developed a lasting affection for the family dog, a borzoi called Toby.

Somewhat to its own surprise, Northampton has proved a fruitful seedbed for British musicians this century, since the town boasts among its sons the names of two other distinguished composers of a similar generation, William Alwyn and Edmund Rubbra, and a composer of the following one, Trevor Hold. In his *Essay in Autobiography*, Edmund Rubbra painted a graphic picture of what life was like in Northampton during his childhood;[2] and though his experiences are not necessarily in direct parallel to those of Arnold, the atmosphere cannot have changed much in the years that separated them. One vital difference, though, was that Arnold's background, thanks to his father's position, was relatively comfortable. Within the family, music already held an established place and he did not have to fight either parental opposition or the middle-class conviction, so resented by Benjamin Britten, that it should never be anything more than a hobby. Arnold was not pressurised into music, but he benefited from a variety of musical experiences from an early age: not just family music-making, such as his mother's singing and playing, but the other sources that, through the 1920s and 1930s, were gradually becoming more widely available, in particular the radio and the gramophone. His first practical involvement, at the age of four, took the form of violin lessons from his aunt Belle, a viola player. Then, when the violin proved too difficult a choice for one of such tender years, he moved on to the piano, with another aunt. As it became evident that the boy had genuine talent, his parents arranged for him to study with the organist of Northampton's most important church, St Matthew's: a link which was eventually to prove useful when a later incumbent, the remarkable Canon Walter Hussey, commissioned Arnold's setting of Psalm 150 at a time in Arnold's life when such requests were not plentiful.

Philip Pfaff, the organist of St Matthew's to whom he was sent, retained Arnold's lasting gratitude for his teaching and encouragement. The composer repaid part of the debt many years later, in 1946, by writing for him the *Festival Overture*, op. 14; Pfaff conducted the first performance that year in Ipswich Town Hall. Arnold has said that he wanted to compose ever since he was a child; recognising this, Pfaff ensured that he had the kind of technical foundation, in harmony and counterpoint, that would serve him in good stead should that ambition be fulfilled.

This strict early grounding found some parallels in Arnold's home life. His father came from a family of Primitive Methodists and the household was suitably respectful. Sundays were strictly observed. In 1971 Arnold told the *Guardian* that 'I was brought up in a very religious household, where you were caned if you refused to go to worship on Sunday'.[3] His parents intended that he should go to Mill Hill, a public school in North London. But this was to result in Malcolm Arnold's first major rebellion against authority. He was already finding school discipline irksome and at the age of thirteen, after a fierce fight, he won the right to stay at home and be tutored by his viola-playing aunt. (Another factor in the decision was his proneness to recurrent bouts of asthma; on more than one occasion, only quick action by his mother saved his life.)

Such a remarkable parental concession to adolescent individuality could partly be explained by the boy's evident musical gifts. But Arnold has also admitted that he was a very spoilt child. His parents believed that if he or any of his brothers or sister showed a particular inclination, it was to be encouraged. The money was there to buy first a drum-kit and then a trumpet, when the desire struck. Later, for his sixteenth birthday in 1937, they bought him an expensive high Bach trumpet.

Methodist strictness was also relaxed in other ways. Family music-making turned increasingly to jazz, then enjoying a huge wave of popularity having left behind its roots in the social protest of Black America. William Arnold used to improvise jazz with a friend. Aubrey Arnold went to Cambridge and found his enthusiasm for jazz stimulated by one of his undergraduate friends, Fred Elizalde, whose name was obviously mentioned around the house in Northampton. Born in the Philippines to wealthy parents and christened Federico, he had been educated in the United States and became known as 'Fred'. At Cambridge in 1926 he founded a band with his brother Manuel called the Quinquaginta Ramblers, which was soon recording for HMV. The following year, Fred Elizalde formed a new band to appear at the Savoy Hotel, an invitation that was short-lived, as his progressive brand of jazz did not wholly suit the clientele who wanted waltzes. He moved on to Spain and was there at the time of the Spanish Civil War, when he supported Franco's Nationalist side. Later, he concentrated on serious composition and on conducting; but as a pioneering figure in the British jazz world during Arnold's formative years Elizalde was always acknowledged by him as a formative influence. Malcolm's sister Ruth, too, became a competent jazz pianist, as well as playing a hybrid instrument called a banjolele; he recalls her party-piece, singing to her own banjolele accompaniment while simultaneously dancing the Charleston. He began to explore her jazz records, responding particularly to the singer Sophie Tucker and the French group with the evocative name of the Quintette du Hot-Club de France, in which Django Reinhardt played the lead guitar – and to Cooty Williams and particularly Louis Armstrong.

An episode involving the great Satchmo was to prove an early catalyst. When Arnold was twelve the family went on holiday to Bournemouth. By chance, Louis Armstrong was due to perform at the Royal Bath Hotel, at a *thé-dansant*. As Arnold waited with his sister in the tea-room, the manager approached and asked if they would mind if Mrs Armstrong sat at their table. The intensity of Louis's playing and singing in 'Sleepy Time Down South', and of Lilian Armstrong's response, left an indelible impression and a strong desire to imitate what he had seen and heard. It led also to an urgent need for the acquisition of a trumpet.

The *Fanfare for Louis* which Arnold wrote in 1970 for a celebration concert in the Queen Elizabeth Hall, and which he inscribed 'For Louis Armstrong's 70th birthday, with admiration and gratitude', was only the most direct of his many homages to the musician who so directly affected his childhood and indeed his entire musical career. The rhythm and swing and infectious *joie de vivre* of Louis at his most exuberant are qualities which reappear regularly in Arnold's music. Without thinking of it in those terms, he absorbed Louis's musical philosophy and attitudes, in particular a desire for immediacy of communication which, without his ever intending such a consequence, was later to set him at odds with the avant-garde. Jazz became for him a corrective, necessary and immediate, to the more serious world of classical music and to the harsher disciplines it imposes. Its rhythms were to permeate Arnold's music throughout his composing career, from the early Clarinet Sonatina of 1951, to the Flute Sonata written in 1977 for James Galway. This obsession with jazz represents many things: escapism and rebellion, but also health, fun, a wider social appeal, and freedom from the tyranny of the written note.

In the early stages, learning the trumpet also meant for Arnold a long apprenticeship. From the age of twelve he had lessons twice a week from a local teacher, again with his mother advising and encouraging. After two years, Mrs Arnold took the teacher aside and bravely asked if the boy had not learned all he could teach him and whether it was not time for a change. And so, at the age of fifteen, supported by a grant from the exhibition fund of the Guildhall School of Music, he was travelling to London for private lessons from Ernest Hall, one of the most celebrated trumpeters of the day. In 1937 he competed for, and won, a scholarship to the Royal College of Music, where Hall was Professor, and was thus able to continue studies with him, as well as broadening his wider musical education.

*

His arrival at the Royal College of Music in South Kensington the following year started on a farcical note. When he identified himself, his name could not be found in any of the lists, until it was discovered that he had been entered as Arnold Malcolm and was presumed to be a relative of the organist George Malcolm. The curriculum required him to pursue four studies: composition and the trumpet were naturally his major interests, but he also took piano and conducting courses.

As a pianist Arnold never made any exaggerated claims for his abilities, describing himself only as 'good enough to accompany people at parties'. At the Royal College he was sent for piano tuition to J. Hurst Bannister, who coached non-keyboard specialists to good effect: Arnold ended up with sufficient skills to try his own music over at the piano when required (though he never composed at the instrument), occasionally to accompany friends or colleagues and to enjoy playing jazz piano, sometimes strumming a bass with his left hand while playing the trumpet with his right. Much later, he told Murray Schafer[4] that he would spend hours improvising at the keyboard, looking for new sounds and harmonies, but that in his view the instrument held its dangers for a composer. Stopping to consider the place of the hands on the keyboard interrupted the musical flow and restricted the shape of a melody. The piano could be deceptive when used as a substitute for the sounds of other instruments, and the composer could only guess at how effects conceived at the keyboard might come off in practice. For these reasons, Arnold forswore the use of the piano as a composing tool at a relatively early age.

Composition was an altogether more serious affair. His first tutor was the formidable Patrick Hadley, later a pillar of music at Cambridge and himself a minor composer in the English pastoral vein. There was an early parting of the ways. As an exercise, Hadley asked Arnold to choose a poem and set it to music. Arnold selected one by his sister Ruth, but did not put her name on the manuscript paper. Hadley was rudely dismissive, not only of the setting but also of the text. Arnold was deeply wounded on both counts and boldly asked for a change. His next tutor was again a respected, even prolific composer: Gordon Jacob, a pupil of Stanford and the author of a much-admired manual on Orchestral Technique. For Arnold, 'Gordon Jacob was marvellous. He let you do free work and would criticise it very thoroughly but in a way that encouraged you. He was very kind and very efficient . . . an inspiring teacher.'[5]

Arnold admired, too, the fact that Gordon Jacob had been something of a hero on the Somme during the First World War, but refused to talk about it. And he was soon to share another attribute: 'Gordon Jacob could write music at any time of the day or night. I used to be a bit like that – able to write music at any time – and that was one of the reasons why I was able to write such a lot.'[6]

Fluency came naturally to the youthful student. He felt sufficiently confident about one early composition, a march for piano written when he was fifteen, to submit it to the publishers Boosey & Hawkes, who declined the offer with their standard rejection letter. A number of other early compositions – including a short song-cycle written in 1938 to poems by Humbert Wolfe – are held in manuscript by the Royal College of Music. Apart from the songs, for the most part they are short piano miniatures, usually dedicated to his mother. In particular, Arnold formed the habit of writing a piece for her birthday on 3 October, rather than buying an unwanted present. Sometimes he tried to incorporate jazz rhythms and influences, struggling to find a notation adequate for the freedom of jazz. Perhaps the most conspicuous example is a fully-fledged ten-minute Piano Sonata in B minor, inscribed 'With love to Mother from Malcolm, Christmas 1942', in which the third movement is an exuberant ragtime finale in march-time. Arnold was quite happy to see this early effort appear in print many years later. His mother lovingly preserved all her son's juvenilia and on her death, on Arnold's birthday in 1956, he went to retrieve them – 'they were the only things I wanted.'[7]

A more serious indication of his composing abilities came towards the end of his second year at the Royal College. A distinguished musical scholar, Walter Wilson Cobbett, had many years earlier endowed an important prize for chamber music. The required composition was to be in the form of a single-movement Fantasy – Cobbett spelled it Phantasy – in one continuous span, but containing a variety of contrasted sections. Arnold submitted a Phantasy for string quartet, and in 1940 was awarded second prize. Later he incorporated part of it into his Wind Quintet, op. 2 (now lost), while the original manuscript is marked in such a way as to imply an intention to transcribe the work for orchestra. Previous winners of the Cobbett Prize, which dated from 1905, had included John Ireland, Herbert Howells, Frank Bridge and Ivor Gurney. A later winner was Benjamin Britten. In such company, Malcolm Arnold had good cause for satisfaction; a composing career was definitely in prospect.

For the moment, though, it was the trumpet which still had pride of place. When Ernest Hall died in August 1984 at the age of ninety-four, Arnold described him as the greatest trumpet teacher there has ever been.

> I was very nervous the first time I went for a lesson with him, but he was very encouraging. He was a wonderful man – a complete human being. Hall was in the London Symphony Orchestra before the 1914 War, and in the King's Private Band – the latter used to exist in those days. After the War he went back to the London Symphony Orchestra, and when the BBC Symphony Orchestra was formed in 1930, he joined them as principal trumpet, where he stayed until he retired. For a short period after the Second War I played as second trumpet alongside him; he wanted me to take over, and was always bitterly disappointed that I gave the trumpet up.[8]

Sitting at the feet of Ernest Hall was not just attractive for sentiment's sake. Hall had not only played under the great conductors of the previous century such as Arthur Nikisch and Hans von Bülow, he had also played for Elgar in the first performance of *Falstaff*, as well as when the composer had conducted the BBC Symphony Orchestra after he had ceased to write any further substantial works. Hall told his young protégé for instance of a notorious passage in the finale of Elgar's Second

Symphony, where he writes a top B natural. One day at rehearsal, Hall had held the note over into the next bar, to thrilling effect, and Elgar so approved that he gave Hall permission to do this every time, even incorporating Hall's alteration in subsequent performances of his own. Arnold learned the trick from his teacher and used it to good effect when the occasion arose. He was thus inheriting in a very real way a particular tradition of orchestral trumpet-playing. Ernest Hall's disappointment when Arnold eventually abandoned the instrument altogether was understandable.

In 1938, though, Arnold's decision to abandon the trumpet lay some years ahead. It had a number of different causes, some of which can be glimpsed even in his College years. He claims to have been disappointed with his own progress – despite the fact that it was now a source of income for him. He undertook his first professional trumpet engagement during the Easter weekend of 1938, when he received seven guineas for playing in the pier orchestra at Llandudno, North Wales. Soon after that he was playing in the pit in the (old) New Theatre in his home town, Northampton, during College vacations. His interest in jazz refused to die down, and while at the Royal College he continued to play Dixieland for dances and at a nearby London pub, the Six Bells in Chelsea. He shared a flat in Caithness Road, off Brook Green in Hammersmith, with a New Zealander called Alex Lindsay, who would sometimes practise his violin all night and then, dressed in a surplice, would go and sing in the choir of the Catholic Church round the corner in the morning. Arnold and Lindsay remained friends until the violinist eventually returned home to a post in the New Zealand Broadcasting Corporation Symphony Orchestra. Another fellow-student, who played in the dance-band Arnold used occasionally to organise, was Arthur Wright. His bass-playing lent a firm foundation to the ensemble – as it was to do for many years in the London Symphony Orchestra after Arthur Wright joined the double bass section.

Relations between music students and landladies were not always easy even then. The percussionist James Blades recalled[9] various unhappy encounters caused by the need to practise, quoting the case of 'a certain landlady who catered for students at the Royal College of Music and who, when Hubert Dawkes – a quiet young man from Dorset – took a late bath on one occasion during his first year of studentship, demanded that Mr Dawkes be found other accommodation, and that she be given a quieter young man in his place. She received one: a new boy – the ebullient Malcolm Arnold.'

One of Arnold's earliest sets of digs in London was at 44 Harcourt Terrace, an establishment presided over by a Miss Needham. Her tolerance of music students was rather greater, but was sometimes tried by renditions of the *Trumpet Voluntary* and other favourites from the trumpet repertoire at hours when such music is not normally heard. Jazz, too, figured significantly in his life – the influence of Fred Elizalde was still strong, as he was now leading a band at the Savoy Hotel and was briefly the darling of London society. Arnold was devouring all kinds of music – in vacations as well as term-time – as well as making use of his piano skills. He went back to his friend and fellow student Jim Aspinall's house in Leicester where the pair tackled the Beethoven symphonies in four-hand versions. He and Donald Swann subjected the Haydn symphonies to similar treatment, often at the house of Alfred Swan – Donald's uncle, though the single 'n' is correct – who was himself something of a composer, and an authority on Russian music.

This pattern of intensely varied musical activity is one that was to be repeated throughout Arnold's life, and, then as now, it brought the desire for occasional escape. When, eventually, Arnold made a break for freedom from the Royal College, it was to the West Country. Early in 1938 he fled London.

> I ran away with a very beautiful Welsh art student with red hair from the Royal College of Art. We went to Plymouth, where I decided never to do music again, and just to live the life of an artisan. But music got the upper hand, and I got a job as a trumpeter in a dance band in Union Street, where I was very happy until I was found by private detectives. My mother and sister came to our room in Monkley Grange, Plymouth, and I explained to my mother that we slept tip-to-toe in bed; of course she did not believe

> me. I picked Plymouth because it was in Devon, and seemed to be a romantic place.[10]

Such gestures of rebellion were nothing new in the Arnold household. His elder sister Ruth had left the Slade School of Fine Art before qualifying, her departure precipitated by riding naked on a carnival float. The offence and the shock were apparently compounded because some of the men on the float were black. With hindsight, it is clear that Ruth Arnold was already showing signs of the instability that was to dog her in later years, before her early death from cancer.

There had been previous incidents, too, involving Malcolm Arnold which had incurred disfavour at the Royal College of Music, including one involving stuffing fish down the organ pipes in the Great Hall; and before his departure for Plymouth, he had also written an abusive letter to the Principal, Sir George Dyson. Dyson was an old-fashioned figure to his students, who derided him for being the author of the standard Army manual on the Mills bomb, or hand grenade. Arnold recalls him as 'long and thin and looking like an El Greco, with a moustache, and hair parted in the middle. But he was very humorous.'[11] Dyson, who is remembered nowadays as a composer mainly for his cantata *The Canterbury Pilgrims*, based on Chaucer, responded in unexpected and enlightened fashion, earning Arnold's subsequent admiration and gratitude. He sent a handwritten reply, saying that the young trumpeter was much needed and much missed, and imploring him to return to take up the place that was waiting for him.

Arnold did so, and for a while his life settled down once more into student routine. His escapade hit the headlines of the national press, caused his eminently respectable and religious parents a great deal of anxiety – and won him a new friend, a flautist, who overcame a natural shyness and introduced himself.

> I was standing in the queue of the College canteen when another student whispered to me that in front was the notorious trumpeter, so I got into conversation with him. This was Malcolm Arnold. He seemed pleased that I had spoken and this meeting led to friendship. He was an odd-looking boy; he had a handsome face,

> but was unattractive-looking because he slouched with his head forward like an old man and turned his feet out as he shambled along, but he was full of jokes and jollity and was the most extrovert and daring person that I had ever met. Among the many friends that I made at College, he became the closest, and we were always laughing, hotly arguing, gossiping, drinking and wandering around London looking at the sights and talking to strangers in pubs and along the way. With him, everything was a lighthearted joke.[12]

This was the flautist Richard Adeney, who went on to a long and distinguished musical career of his own, as both soloist and orchestral player. The friendship between the two men was cemented by their mutual respect for each other's playing. As they rubbed shoulders in the venerable corridors of the Royal College of Music, Richard Adeney quickly formed a vivid impression of his new-found friend. He was interested in the possibility of travel, and of seeing new and unfamiliar places. Politically, Malcolm Arnold was inclined to be left-wing, and in sympathy with the pacifist movement. Adeney found him full of humour, already sceptical about his future profession – with a specially keen eye for the pretensions of conductors – but with the ability still to be moved by great music. Music came easily to him: due to meet Adeney's younger sister, whose cello studies had not progressed as far as her brother's trumpet-playing, Arnold quickly sketched a miniature Trio for flute, trumpet (muted) and cello (easy), which the threesome played through informally.

Richard Adeney's father ran an art school which in 1940, as a result of the war, was moved out to Arnold's home town of Northampton. As a result, the two students were thrown together in vacations as well as term-time.

> We got up a concert in the Town Hall, for which he wrote most of the music under various pseudonyms; for instance, his new flute sonata was in the programme as 'Sonate poor flute, by A. Youngman' (the word 'pour' being deliberately misspelt). It was rather good and I wonder where it is now; perhaps lying in some dusty Northampton attic. As the local paper had no music critic, I wrote a review of it myself. For a joke, I slated the concert, criticising especially strongly my own playing, and friends who had

> been in the audience were outraged, one even saying that I should sue the paper.[13]

And yet the friendship was an unlikely one. Adeney was cautious and insecure, uncertain of his sexual orientation, and a convinced pacifist. There were sides to his friend's character of which he did not approve. One in particular was to be prophetic:

> Malcolm believed in the glamour of drunkenness and the supremacy of youth; he said that he was going to kill himself at thirty, for he had no intention of becoming a dreadful, boring old man.[14]

The year after the Plymouth incident, the lure of the West Country again proved irresistible. Arnold, taking Richard Adeney with him, spent an idyllic holiday in Cornwall, even as all-out war loomed. With them to Hope Cove went also an attractive girl named Betty Coleman, the daughter of a Bournemouth doctor. Arnold took along some music for them to play together, another miniature trio, ironically headed *Suite Bourgeoise*, for flute, trumpet and piano – Betty Coleman was, in Arnold's opinion, a brilliant piano accompanist. He remained very fond of her, kept in touch until she married a violinist and later became godfather to her son Timothy. He sent a silver napkin ring for the christening, but was unable to attend, being detained, neither for the first nor the last time, by the urgent business of completing a film score to a deadline.

The Cornwall holiday marked a watershed in another way. In that summer of 1940, it seemed more than possible that Hitler's forces would cross the Channel, land in Dorset, and cut off the West Country from the rest of England. No wonder the threesome seemed to have Cornwall to themselves, even while feeling that time was not on their side. No wonder each was restless, Arnold most of all. Back at the College during the Blitz, along with his fellow-students, he was given firewatching duties. He passed some of these often tedious periods of watching and waiting by playing chess, one of his current passions, sometimes through the night with the renowned violinist Albert Sammons, who after a long career as a soloist and in the London orchestras was now a professor of violin at the College.

Then came a major and unexpected change: before the end of his second year at Prince Consort Road and despite the compositional achievement of the Cobbett Prize, Arnold was offered – and accepted – the position of second trumpet in the London Philharmonic Orchestra. This time he did leave, for good, without taking the exam for a formal qualification. When, years later, he was made an FRCM – Fellow of the Royal College of Music – he remarked that it was much better than being a mere ARCM, the qualification he had never achieved. On the BBC's *Desert Island Discs* he told Roy Plomley jokingly that the College still owed him a year of his scholarship!

So, before he was twenty, Malcolm Arnold joined the ranks of one of the great orchestras. The demands of front-rank public exposure, and of comparison with his peers, were therefore added to the virtuoso demands of his chosen instrument before he came of age.

The London Philharmonic was no ordinary musical institution. The history of its early years is unique and certainly coloured Arnold's views about self-help and social organisation during the eight years he was associated with it. Founded by Sir Thomas Beecham in 1934, the LPO still retained the impact of his personality, as Thomas Russell recalled,[15] despite Beecham's illness and departure for America at the start of the war. This had precipitated a crisis, a threat to the Orchestra's existence that was only overcome by Russell's insistence that the musicians form themselves into what was virtually a self-governing co-operative, with a uniquely democratic structure. Originally a string-player, Russell eventually became General Manager of the LPO, masterminding the celebrated *Musical Manifesto* of 1940 which, over the signature of J. B. Priestley, launched the orchestra's fight for survival. Arnold had even attended the linked Manifesto Concert as a student. Shortly before he joined, the Orchestra suffered a further heavy blow with the loss of many valuable instruments in the bombing of Queen's Hall in May 1941.

During the War, the London Philharmonic's decision to continue its activities under a management committee drawn from its own members was a brave one. They raised enough support to carry on in this fashion for the duration of hostilities; but it often meant that the players had to suffer financially, fees being limited to a share in whatever was left after all expenses had been paid. Their resolve to remain self-governing after the war was, if anything, even braver, as it effectively discouraged the return to his former position of Sir Thomas Beecham, together with the financial stability his presence might have been expected to bring with it.

The first concert Arnold played with the LPO, in the Miners' Hall, Rhôs, Wrexham, was conducted by the great Austrian tenor Richard Tauber, whose abilities in this field Arnold rated highly. The LPO had no Principal Conductor for much of the time that Arnold was a member, partly at Thomas Russell's insistence. Instead there were regular visitors. During the war the most notable of them was Leslie Heward, who was to die young. (Much later, in the composer's crisis years, Heward's daughter Karen was to prove a friend.) Constant Lambert, whom Arnold knew from Royal College days, also made regular appearances.

> I used to play in the second orchestra there for his conductor's class, and then later when I became a professional orchestral musician I would meet him for a drink at the Nag's Head in St Martin's Lane, a lovely old pub. He was a lovely man, but strangely he was sometimes inhibited on the rostrum. When he gave himself a free rein he could do some really good performances.[16]

Constant Lambert was sixteen years older than Malcolm Arnold, and by the time Arnold first set eyes on him he was already a public figure, in particular through his work with the Sadler's Wells Ballet. There were parallels between the two men which neither knew about, but which with hindsight did not bode well for Arnold. Lambert, too, had been precocious, leaving school young to go as a student to the Royal College of Music. Early on, he also had been fixated on jazz, but he had matured early. In the College and at art galleries and theatres his limping figure suggested to his friends self-containment and forthrightness in equal proportions. He impressed everyone with his wide knowledge of the arts, his musical scholarship and with his decisiveness. He easily combined his pursuit of knowledge with his appetite for fun, and somehow reconciled them with the constraints of having to return home each night to his mother's house.[17]

If there was less of the rebel in the young Constant Lambert than in the young Arnold, other similarities were strong: the dominant mother, the enjoyment of pubs and clubs and soon, a tension between composing and performing – one which Lambert for his part never satisfactorily resolved. A love of ballet, too, was soon to be common to them both. And Lambert, though he was destined as a composer to remain a peripheral figure in English musical history, remembered only for *The Rio Grande* and a couple of his ballets, made an enduring impression on the younger man as a theorist. His book *Music, Ho!* – the title is from Shakespeare, and the line that follows, unquoted by Lambert, is poignant:

Leave it alone; let's to billiards –

was first published in 1934 and has seldom been out of print since. It covers an immense amount of ground, and some of it is doubtless wish-fulfilment of what Lambert was unable to achieve in his own music. Many of the judgements and prophecies seem, half a century or more afterwards, to be wildly mistaken. Nevertheless, the final chapters in particular struck a particular chord with Arnold, where Lambert sets out the case for Sibelius as representing the music of the future. Coming after a sequence where he has considered and rejected many alternatives, such as Stravinsky, Schoenberg and Hindemith, Lambert's espousal of Sibelian rigour and discipline is almost messianic in its powerful rhetoric. Arnold's worship of Sibelius, and his reverence for the symphony as the highest form of musical art, owe a great deal to *Music, Ho!*, and to the charisma of Lambert's personality, and the latter's death at the age of forty-six cut short a potential partnership of much promise. Arnold wept at the news.

After the war, other regular visitors to the LPO included Anatole Fistoulari, Alceo Galliera, Jean Martinon and Eduard van Beinum, the last being appointed Chief Conductor in 1948. Van Beinum's concerts with the orchestra regularly included Mahler and Bruckner, often performed to near-empty houses, but they gave Arnold his first contact with this music. Others under whom he was to perform in due course included Bruno Walter, Erich Kleiber, Ernest Ansermet, Sergiu Celibidache, Adrian Boult and Clemens Krauss. He played under Furtwängler for a Decca recording of Brahms's Second Symphony, and under Victor de Sabata for a recording of the *Eroica* Symphony of Beethoven. And he took part in the first British performance, with Jascha Heifetz as the soloist, of the Violin Concerto by William Walton, later to become his closest musical friend.

Arnold therefore learned the great symphonic repertoire from the inside, sitting in an orchestra under some of the greatest conductors of the day. He regarded it as a vital component of his musical education. He also discovered that orchestral players, then as now, had to be familiar with every variety of commercial music as well. Although at home in Northampton he had listened to records not just of jazz but of, first, what he called 'highly-coloured music', meaning particularly Stravinsky and Delius, then the Baroque composers, particularly Bach and Vivaldi, and had finally arrived at Beethoven, within the LPO the range of music he played and heard was infinitely greater. Membership of Beecham's brainchild brought with it exciting discoveries: 'It was after the LPO had played a movement of Mahler's Second Symphony that he rushed off to Foyle's Bookshop to buy all the Mahler scores he could lay his hands on. During the long *tacets* which fall to the lot of all brass players, he had the leisure to listen, and to discover at first hand what worked and what didn't work in matters of instrumentation.'[18]

This was just the beginning of his long love-affair with Mahler's music – which was soon bolstered by a further unexpected encounter. 'I lived in a mews in Bayswater then, and one day with the window open I was playing the slow movement of the Fourth

Symphony on the piano. I stopped because my fingers got muddled up and a woman's voice outside carried on the melody. I looked out. She was a sculptor who lived up the road, and I said, "Do you know what this is?" "Of course I do," she said, "my father wrote it."'[19] Anna Mahler was indeed then eking out a precarious living in London as a refugee.

Arnold joined the LPO in the first place because the principal trumpet, Richard Walton, was serving in the forces. John Cozens moved up to take that position and Arnold sat alongside him, learning all the time. Cozens told him of places in orchestral scores where conductors expected and sanctioned alterations – another example of the orchestral traditions he had previously learned about from Ernest Hall. Within a year Cozens left and Malcolm Arnold, just twenty-one, found himself at the start of 1943 Principal Trumpet of the London Philharmonic – and wondering before long if he, too, was in the wrong place.

There were two reasons for the dilemma. The first was the unresolved struggle between playing and composing. In wartime, composing for a living was not a practical proposition, but this did not lessen the frustration. Arnold also found that playing great music did not diminish but actually fostered the urge to write and forced him to think in particular about musical form. How important was melody? Was development essential? How did you resolve matters at the end? He needed to write and to experiment, to find the answers to the musical questions that had begun increasingly to preoccupy him.

The second reason for his uncertainty was the war itself. It is no exaggeration to say that Malcolm Arnold's war began in comedy, passed through hopeless muddle and ended on a note of tragedy and – literally – pain, as he eventually turned a gun on himself in frustration.

2 : Concerto for Trumpet

or *Tiger in the Smoke*

At the outbreak of the Second World War Malcolm Arnold was within six weeks of his eighteenth birthday. He had been appalled as an impressionable adolescent by the tragedy and human suffering of the Spanish Civil War. Like many another student at this time of tension and uncertainty his inclinations were towards pacifism. Under the initial call-up regulations the exemption age was under twenty-seven, and he was able to continue his musical studies, combining them with occasional turns of duty in the Fire Service. Eventually, however, as the situation changed, he received his call-up papers and determined to register as a conscientious objector.

The intellectual climate of this period was one of intense debate on matters of war and militarism. Writers and public figures often declared their position uncompromisingly. Arnold had read, for example, Erich Maria Remarque's *All Quiet on the Western Front* and the writings of Bernard Shaw, Vera Brittain and George Lansbury. He listened regularly to the broadcasts of Dick Sheppard and noted the anti-war views of another influential figure, Canon Charles Raven, the Master of Christ's College Cambridge. People took sides vigorously over Mahatma Gandhi.

Arnold's decision to register, as his friend Richard Adeney had done, as a conscientious objector took courage in itself. Such registration was by no means a comfortable experience – often it was just the opposite. In particular there was the likelihood of opprobrium from those who took a different view. Muddle in the public mind over the nuances between conscientious objection to conscription or military involvement, easily construed as cowardice, as against outright pacifism, led to a generalised lack of sympathy towards those who objected. The relevant legislation now seems enlightened – efforts were evidently made to avoid the appearance of head-on clashes between conscientious objectors and the state – but at the time there was no escaping the suggestion of stigma. Arnold felt it too. Is it, perhaps, in some part responsible for his later change of mind and his eventual decision to join up? Many reasons suggest themselves and interlock, however; and none predominates. He duly appeared before a conscientious objection tribunal on 20 March 1941 in Nottingham, where the Midlands area sittings were held. The presiding officer, Judge Longson, and two fellow commissioners found in Arnold's favour, on condition that he pursued his musical activities. It came as a shock to him to read in the paper that Judge Longson had died the day after the tribunal hearing.

Malcolm Arnold thus returned, aged nineteen, from the ordeal of the hearing to his varied musical activities. Within a year, though, constrained by the difficulties of wartime orchestral life, frustrated in his growing desire to compose, devastated by the loss of his brother Philip, killed in the RAF, and shaken by some of the defeatism he encountered in the capital, he had reversed his earlier decision. Malcolm Arnold was now determined to enlist. 'I had exemption as a conscientious objector, not the Christian pacifist sort but an aggressive one, yet I joined the Army. My views which were totally cynical turned out to be correct.'[1]

Arnold would have preferred the Navy, but in 1944 there was no space. He volunteered for the Buffs and underwent a full infantry training. Then, thanks to a classic example of Army insensitivity, he was put in the Regimental Band. The former first trumpet of the LPO found himself not fighting the Nazis but playing parade-ground marches and selections from Gilbert and Sullivan on the cornet for the entertainment of officers.

This time his protest took a more extreme form: ultimate authority meant ultimate rebellion. Exhausted, frustrated and angry at what he saw as a deliberate humiliation, he shot a hole through his naked foot with his army rifle.

> I am not particularly proud of that. It was very painful, and there was a lot of blood around. The man who had been giving us bayonet practice found me and fainted. I was left alone for some time before the medical officer arranged for a stretcher party, and I went to hospital. I was then discharged with no blemish on my character.[2]

Arnold spent a month in hospital and eventually, early in 1945, was invalided out of the Army and enabled to return to playing the trumpet. In his unpublished memoirs, Richard Adeney makes the point in connection with Malcolm Arnold that shooting oneself in wartime is a capital offence, because it represents a form of desertion. Arnold was extremely fortunate to find himself in the hands of a sympathetic psychologist, who did all he could to get him out of the Army. The consequences could have been a great deal more severe than they were. For a short time he joined the BBC Symphony Orchestra, where he found himself playing next to his old mentor, Ernest Hall. But the BBC's original second trumpet soon returned from the war and reclaimed his old job: as Arnold discovered one morning when Adrian Boult met him in the Maida Vale studios and expressed his regret that they would 'not be seeing much more of one another'. Arnold then resumed his position as first trumpet with his old orchestra, the London Philharmonic. He was to stay with the LPO until 1948.

The Army episode raises all kinds of questions, some of which are difficult to answer satisfactorily. It came as the culmination of an extraordinary sequence of changes of mind: his initial reluctance to serve his country; his first joining the LPO, then leaving it a year later to enlist; rapidly followed by the realisation that this was a catastrophic mistake and that Army life, with its inherent sadistic and authoritarian sides, was intolerable; finally a return to orchestral routine which, if he had previously sometimes enjoyed it for its performing and sociable aspects, he had also found irksome and frustrating to his desire to compose. Had he been an officer in possession of a revolver, head rather than foot might have been the target. Whatever psychological parallels might be drawn between this self-mutilating gesture and later similar assaults on himself – and also with the emotional contours of some of his music – there is here, too, the seed of a recurrent musical theme: human freedom set against the tyranny of war and of mindless institutions. (Arnold was later to write the music for the St Trinian's films, where anarchy rules supreme.) This streak of anti-authoritarianism, apparent in his school days – or lack of them – and now again in the Army, was to permeate his musical preoccupations and style, and eventually at times his mission as a composer. It is present in the very first of Malcolm Arnold's works to win him widespread recognition: the Overture, *Beckus the Dandipratt*.

Beckus was written in 1943, before the Army episode. The Overture includes, ironically, a prominent part for the cornet, which depicts an urchin (the 'dandipratt' of the title) in whom Arnold's inner ear evidently heard himself as soloist. Beckus is, if not a rebel, then certainly an outcast, and in a dignified symphony orchestra, the cornet (= Malcolm Arnold) is something of a grubby visitor. Beckus is also clearly a linear descendant of another rather older musical urchin, one who came to a sticky end: Richard Strauss's *Till Eulenspiegel*, a work Arnold programmed on more than one occasion when he became active for a time as a conductor.

Arnold is not, however, the cornet soloist on the first recording of the work (made by Decca five years later in 1948) which represented an enormous piece of good fortune for the composer and constituted his first real breakthrough. The London Philharmonic, to which Arnold had returned, was recording the Third Symphony of Brahms under the Dutchman Eduard van Beinum. The orchestra knew the work well, the conductor was one of the best organised in the business and – a rare occurrence in the studio then or later – the recording was finished with time in hand. The question arose as to how the spare session should be filled.

> Van Beinum knew of my overture *Beckus the Dandipratt*, for I had shown him the score . . . He suggested to the producer, Victor Olof, that we record my overture; and to my great surprise and delight, he agreed. And so I came to play on this recording. Actually the recording quality was of demonstration standard, and this record was often used as a test record for equipment.[3]

Richard Adeney was led to believe that Arnold had previously given the score of *Beckus the Dandipratt* to Sir Henry Wood for consideration, after he had conducted the LPO. Some time later the score was returned with a note of refusal. Arnold thought Wood had scarcely bothered to look at it, claiming to have marked several pages with tape which had not been disturbed.

The recording of *Beckus the Dandipratt* in 1948 was, though, no shot in the dark – or in the foot – by Decca. The five years since the Army episode had seen Arnold gradually beginning to establish a reputation amid the rubble of artistic life during and after the war.

The roots of this early achievement go back even further, to his first period in the LPO before he volunteered for the Buffs. Despite his youth, Arnold had settled in rapidly during 1941 and made some lasting musical friendships. Orchestral life in wartime meant a great deal of touring, endless slow train journeys, long periods of boredom. As in any such body, the players relieved the tedium with occasional sessions of chamber music. These provided Arnold with an obvious outlet for his composing instincts and with a means of whiling away the hours by writing music. With the encouragement of some of his fellow players he wrote first of all a Wind Quintet for the five woodwind principals of the LPO: the flautist Richard Adeney, the oboist Michael Dobson, the clarinettist John Clucas, the horn-player Charles Gregory and the bassoonist George Alexandra. It was performed first in London in June 1943 at a concert mounted by the Committee for the Promotion of New Music. That score, sadly, is lost. Richard Adeney, who admired the piece, thought the culprit was Dennis Brain, when he borrowed the parts. As a result we can only guess at what it was like.

It was followed by an increasing number of pieces for chamber music combinations, beginning with another work for wind quintet whose enduring freshness has guaranteed it a permanent place in the repertoire. The *Three Shanties*, op. 4, received an unlikely first outing in an aircraft hangar. They were first heard at Filton Aerodrome in Bristol, in August 1943, during a lunchtime shift – a scene memorably recreated in Kriss Rusmanis's seventieth birthday film about Malcolm Arnold for BBC Television's *Omnibus* series. The *Shanties* are still deservedly popular for their high spirits, virtuoso demands and sheer inventiveness. Although each of the three very brief movements is based on a sea-shanty – respectively 'What shall we do with the drunken sailor?', 'Boney was a Warrior' and 'Johnny come down to Hilo' – these are much more than mere arrangements. Both the quick outer movements subject their chosen tune to all manner of distortions, rhythmic and harmonic: the treatment is light-hearted and tongue-in-cheek, after the manner of, say, Stravinsky in his Octet. The youthful Arnold finds in his chosen themes more sheer music than one would ever expect – so, for instance, the central shanty, with its muted horn solo at the outset, is magically transformed into a twilit, gently lapping seascape.

Such occasional pieces were almost the rule rather than the exception and as a trumpeter Malcolm Arnold once or twice found himself on the receiving end. The LPO's bass clarinet was Richard Temple Savage, somewhat older than Arnold, who was supplementing his income by acting as the orchestra's wartime librarian. His autobiography provides a vivid picture of music-making in wartime, and of the circumstances behind the creation of an occasional piece of his own:

> I was as usual busy copying, and my hotel had no long table; so I had taken to going down to the Colston Hall in Bristol during the day where I could find one to my liking. A strange assortment of instrumentalists seemed to be practising there: a trumpet (Malcolm Arnold), a flute (Richard Adeney), a viola (Wrayburn Glasspool) and a bassoon (George Alexandra). My exasperation at this odd combination led me to compose *Five Foolish Fancies* for them, subtitled 'On Tour' and comprising an 'Overture to a Reluctant Landlady', a limping March called 'Looking for Digs', a Waltz 'No Rehearsal', and a Dirge – 'No Beer'. The fifth number has passed from my recollection, and the score has long been lost.[4]

The Dirge in particular struck a sympathetic chord with the trumpeter! Meanwhile, the success of Arnold's own *Three Shanties* was swift, and it had a lot to do with their relaxed, non-experimental character. It took some time for Arnold to recognise that this was a fruitful vein; and some of his other music from this early period, again written for friends in the LPO, shows him trying out new ideas less comfortably. Another Quintet, this time for the unlikely combination of flute, violin, viola, horn and bassoon, has a middle movement that is essentially a study in textures, with no thematic material to speak of. Instead it suggests another influence – the tolling monotone in 'Le Gibet' from Maurice Ravel's *Gaspard de la Nuit* – as does the slow movement of a Trio, again for friends in the LPO and scored for the improbable combination of flute, viola and bassoon. In its sinewy textures there are echoes of yet another possible influence on the still impressionable Arnold, that of Gustav Holst, whose presence is particularly evident in the lively final jig.

Even when the war ended, friends in the orchestra continued to be an obvious source of inspiration. The early Horn Concerto no. 1 of 1945 must be one of the few such pieces from this period of British musical history not written for Dennis Brain. Instead, Arnold composed it for Charles Gregory, first horn of the LPO. In 1948 his close friend from the Royal College of Music, the flautist Richard Adeney, who had joined the LPO shortly before Arnold in 1942 and been there ever since, received the first of his several dedications, the Flute Sonatina, op. 19. A colleague in the trumpet section, Eric Bravington, who later became the Orchestra's long-serving General Manager, cemented their friendship in a different way by inviting Arnold to be best man at his wedding in 1943. A year later, a member of the LPO first violins, John Kuchmy, who also played the piano more than passably, inspired a piano work. In deference to his origins, it was called *Variations on a Ukrainian Folk Song*, op. 9, although the tune sounds suspiciously like a popular song of the day called 'Yes my darling daughter'. Yet the piece is serious, one of Arnold's most self-consciously modernist scores, with barely a key-signature in sight and a percussiveness and angularity in the writing that suggest two more influences, Bartók or Prokofiev.

Conductors inevitably loomed large in his musical experiences at this period. First and foremost Malcolm Arnold reserved his admiration for Sir Thomas Beecham, and rather surprisingly for Beecham as a technician. Beecham's beat, he maintained, gave the clearest possible indication of the way the conductor wanted the music to sound. The baton alone could and should produce the suavity of Mozart, the fire of Berlioz, and all the necessary lightning-fast contrasts of articulation, mood and character. Though the LPO had formed itself into a self-governing collective during the war, according to Arnold the orchestra's manager Thomas Russell was at least partially concerned to 'keep the LPO suitable for Beecham', in the hope he might return to what was, after all, his creation. This was the reason many players had joined in the first place, out of admiration or respect.

There were indeed new faces in the LPO at this period, and the sheer quantity of them may have had something to do with the parting of the ways between Beecham and the orchestra, which largely took place during Arnold's period away in the army and at the BBC Symphony. The conductor returned from the United States to his old orchestra amid high hopes; but as Richard Temple Savage, who played regularly for him, comments: 'Beecham always needed players who understood him.'[5] There were constant niggles; relations with the idiosyncratic Thomas Russell who had held the fort so bravely during Sir Thomas's absence were often uneasy, with the orchestra often unwilling to surrender the limited amount of democracy it had acquired in those years, and generally the old magic was gone. There was no sudden parting of the ways, but the relationship slowly shrivelled and in 1946 Beecham formed a new orchestra, the Royal Philharmonic, which was to be the glory of his final years. Malcolm Arnold, however, despite his continuing admiration for the conductor, did not follow him to his new enterprise, preferring to stay loyal to the LPO.

Thomas Russell's policy for the orchestra affected every aspect of its life, but especially choice of repertoire, selection of new players – and invitations to conductors. Thus Arnold was able to observe the likes of Ernest Ansermet, Victor de Sabata, and a rising young star from the USA in the shape of Leonard Bernstein.

Bernstein visited the LPO in June 1946. It was a deeply unhappy experience for all concerned. Bernstein's own account, offered almost half a century later, suggests a number of mitigating circumstances. London was going through a freak cold spell. He could not buy a pair of gloves or a sweater. There were no acceptable concert halls functioning and the Stoll Theatre was acoustically inadequate. He was ill with a fever. There was no publicity. The ailing conductor lay in the Hyde Park Hotel feeling at death's door while the Army had to scour the country for penicillin for him. He was indeed on the point of withdrawing, and replacements were approached. As for the LPO: 'The orchestra was half-demobilised only, the soldiers hadn't come back from Army service yet, so it was not very good . . . The orchestra couldn't play in tune because there were so many substitutes . . . I can't tell you how hard I worked, especially on *Appalachian Spring* to try to get the piece learned.'[6]

Yet at least one Bernstein concert did in the event take place as planned in a packed Royal Albert Hall, and the review in *The Times* was not unenthusiastic, recognising in the young man a gifted Wagner conductor – the soprano Marjorie Lawrence sang the closing scene from *Götterdämmerung* – and praising a vivid performance of Walton's *Portsmouth Point* Overture and the quality and individuality of the Copland ballet.

In Arnold's memory, the Bernstein rehearsals did not proceed at all smoothly, the American's brashness, even arrogance, upsetting the veterans in the orchestra. The American cried off from one out-of-town concert – ostensibly because of illness but Arnold thought it was diplomatic – and Eduard van Beinum stepped into the breach. He happened to be in London on non-musical business: the Dutch being a nation of cyclists but bicycles being in short supply after the war he had come over to search for a suitable machine.

From the trumpet desk Arnold observed, and admired, a master at work and from this encounter emerged the 1948 *Beckus* recording. Another encounter was also auspicious: a performance by the LPO of William Walton's Overture, *Scapino*, under the baton of the composer himself, with Arnold and his friend Sidney Ellison playing the difficult trumpet parts. Again, the acquaintanceship was to develop into a significant musical friendship.

Other friendships arose through activities away from the orchestra. In 1943 he took part in a brass concert at St Peter's Church, Eaton Square in London. For it, he arranged a couple of pieces of thirteenth- and fourteenth-century music for brass trio, including Guillaume de Machaut's celebrated Double Hoquet. In Arnold's arrangement, the bumpy rhythms implied by the title became even more pronounced, but were taken in their stride by the trio, which included a brilliant young horn-player called Dennis Brain. This encounter was the start of a friendship that lasted until Brain's death some fourteen years later. His biographer records that, when the pair later performed the Machaut arrangement for the BBC, 'they were both so struck by the humour of the piece that they had to stand back to back in the studio to avoid breaking into laughter.'[7]

Another excursion outside the LPO took Arnold under the umbrella, for the brief period of its existence, of the Rudolf Dolmetsch Orchestra. He played first trumpet in this chamber-sized group, appearing with some regularity at the Aeolian Hall, a location which had achieved notoriety a few years earlier as the scene of the first-night riot during William Walton's *Façade*. The ensemble was a sad casualty of the war: Rudolf Dolmetsch, the eldest of Arnold Dolmetsch's children and an exceptionally gifted musician in his own right, was killed tragically young.

One wartime engagement which particularly stuck in the young trumpeter's memory was an appearance at the Wigmore Hall on 7 May 1943. The programme was part of an extended series designed as a gesture of support for the Free French Government and was planned by Felix Aprahamian, then on the staff of the LPO, later a respected critic, to include a number of popular French pieces such as Fauré's *Dolly Suite*, 'The Swan' from Saint-Saëns's *Carnival of the Animals*, and Bizet's *Jeux d'Enfants*. The artists were a mixture of British and French: Huguette Vivers, Gaston Richer, Howard Ferguson, Denis Matthews. The climax of the concert was a performance of Saint-Saëns's Septet for piano, string quintet and trumpet. Arnold thus found himself playing alongside a number of distinguished contemporaries on an occasion whose significance was reinforced by the news, just in, of Allied successes in the western desert of North Africa. Relief and euphoria were in the air and Arnold recalled that his mastery of spoken French knew no bounds that night!

The war also saw the emergence of the aspiring composer's first orchestral works, the *Beckus* Overture and, immediately before it, a tone poem called *Larch Trees*, op. 3. As its uncharacteristic title implies, it used a different manner altogether and was a somewhat faltering first step, the heavy imprint of Delius subduing Arnold's natural voice. At the time, Arnold was heavily under the spell of Beecham's recordings for the Delius Society. But *Larch Trees* was at least heard and noticed, for it was performed at the very first private 'Experimental Rehearsal' of new orchestral works mounted by the Committee for the Promotion of New Music, and it benefited from the attendant publicity. At this stage in his career Arnold had no publisher, no orchestral material and no copyist. The parts were therefore copied by the composer himself and his viola-playing friend from the LPO, Wrayburn Glasspool. The performance took place on a Friday afternoon, 1 October 1943, with the LPO led by Jean Pougnet, at no less a venue than the Royal Albert Hall, since the Queen's Hall had by now been flattened by a bomb. Arnold's was one of three works[8] to be rehearsed publicly and then performed: he was the only composer to conduct his own piece. After the concert, in a display of musical democracy that sounds daring even today, a vote was taken to determine which of the three works should be repeated and an open forum was also held in one of the smaller rooms off the hall. The driving force behind the Committee was another composer, Francis Chagrin, who had already initiated the series of chamber recitals where other Arnold pieces had been heard, and his intention was to bring the music being played to the attention of agents, critics, publishers and promoters of music such as the BBC. *Larch Trees* won the vote.

Despite such brave ventures, when the war ended British music was effectively faced with the task of finding itself again. The deaths of Elgar, Holst and Delius within the same year (1934) had left a gap that had still to be filled, with only the powerful but unique figure of Ralph Vaughan Williams enjoying a secure reputation. There was still a formidable musical Establishment: apart from Vaughan Williams, there were composers of the older generation still living such as Arnold Bax, Arthur Bliss, Gerald Finzi and John Ireland. Arnold was aware of the emergence of a post-war British school, identifying not as might be expected the names of Britten and Tippett, but Peter Racine Fricker and Alan Rawsthorne, in both of whom (unlike Britten and Tippett) the symphonic instinct was strong. Not surprisingly, Malcolm Arnold's own early efforts as a composer were eventually to culminate in a First Symphony, written during 1948 and completed the following February. The path to it, however, was a hard one.

Arnold's apprenticeship consisted of some twenty compositions, in the course of which he was slowly but surely to find his true voice as a composer. On the way to the First Symphony, there were a number of milestones, personal as well as musical. In 1941 he married for the first time. Sheila Nicholson was a violinist pupil of the distinguished teacher Marjorie Hayward at the Royal Academy of Music in Euston Road, where she won the coveted Dove Prize. Not wanting to lose touch with music, in addition to leading the local orchestra in Richmond, Surrey, where the couple soon moved, Sheila Arnold continued to play for a time in the Riddick String Orchestra; an association that led to the commissioning by Kathleen Riddick of Arnold's Symphony for Strings, op. 13, and to its first performance by her orchestra in Kensington Town Hall in April 1947. Sheila Arnold also taught a good deal and her husband was sometimes to complain that it was impossible to obtain at 19 Denbigh Gardens the peace and quiet he needed for composition. Eventually there was a further source of conflict: Arnold did not get on too happily with his mother-in-law, who was Welsh and a forceful character in her own right.

At the start, though, these troubles lay over the horizon. In 1948 their daughter Katherine was born, followed by a son,

Robert, two years later. The year before, Arnold had at last acquired his first publisher, Alfred Lengnick & Co., based in Purley, Surrey, with whom he was to remain for some five years. Lengnick not only printed the chamber pieces which he continued to write – in particular, sonatas for violin and viola, the latter written for the leading player of the day, Frederick Riddle – but also encouraged him in other directions. So the *Children's Suite*, op. 16, for piano, though of elementary simplicity, contains recognisable Arnold touches of melody and harmony, while sticking closely to its technical brief: six Studies for such matters as trills, or legato thirds in the left hand.

Apart from writing music for children he also became involved with young music-making more directly, through a meeting with Ruth Railton, who was to play a key role in his struggles to establish himself as a professional composer. Aware of a significant gap in British musical institutions, she had set about the creation of a National Youth Orchestra, seeking out funds, borrowing music and rehearsal space, fixing up auditions nationwide, arranging tours and concerts, enlisting the practical support of soloists and orchestral players. It was almost inevitable that Arnold, still young and enthusiastic and active both as composer and performer, should become involved. Ruth Railton's memoirs paint a vivid if somewhat exaggerated picture.

> A few months earlier I had met a young trumpet player from the London Philharmonic Orchestra. He wanted to compose, and responded at once to the idea of a first performance at our first concert. His eyes shone, he radiated warmth and enthusiasm. When I explained that I hadn't yet got an orchestra, that the potential talent was only elementary in performance, that most members would never have played in a symphony orchestra, he laughed and said 'All the better!' There was not much time, but he would write a Suite, would see to the copying of the parts, and would come to Bath to help the young brass players. Rumour has it that he went back to the LPO, threw down his trumpet and left to be a composer.[9]

In 1948 Arnold wrote the first of several National Youth Orchestra works; this one bore the title *To Youth*, though it was published eight years later simply as Little Suite no. 1. The Suite was duly heard for the first time in the Assembly Rooms, Bath, at the first concert given by the National Youth Orchestra of Great Britain on 21 April 1948, when it shared the platform with works by Mozart, Beethoven, Weber and Elgar. When he attended rehearsals, Ruth Railton found him to be an inspiring teacher.

> He explained that the young know when things are wrong, but can't always analyse why, and teachers are vague and don't tell them. They say, 'Do it again' or 'Practise it'. 'Tell them it's sharp,' said Malcolm, 'and they'll put it right; or that those actual notes were too slow; and they'll respond at once. Teaching is telling them what they don't know.' The experienced performer has often forgotten the obvious and the simple, and has to rediscover or remember what it is that young players don't yet know and don't yet hear.[10]

Ruth Railton's instinct that Malcolm Arnold was destined to be a natural partner of the National Youth Orchestra was abundantly borne out, not only in the Divertimento and the three Little Suites for young players that came later, but also in his involvement with the Orchestra in more direct ways. He took part in some of the earliest auditions, and undertook coaching duties during the residential periods, mostly in school holidays, when the repertoire, old and new, was mastered and the groundwork laid for the NYO's enduring success. Ruth Railton benefited too: 'I learned most from Malcolm Arnold: so talented, full of ideas, imagination and humour, with the warmest, most generous personality.'[11]

For all this involvement, though, Arnold never became a committed teacher in the way that many of his colleagues and contemporaries did, either then or later. Once the composing career took off, there was the matter of time, an increasingly scarce commodity. But his instincts were against it as well: a feeling that, while the technical essentials are a matter of strict discipline, musicianship and inspiration are either innate or not. Arnold did not enjoy teaching the trumpet; he had effectively abandoned the instrument professionally by the age of twenty-seven. He did, though, teach the trumpet to the daughter of J. B. Priestley for a time.

When the National Youth Orchestra gave its first overseas concert, in Paris in 1950, Ruth Railton asked him for a new piece. 'With his usual generosity and enthusiasm he responded at once. He thought a Divertimento, with different movements to show our various qualities and use the full strength of the orchestra, would be best; and he would come with us to Paris.'[12]

The concert duly took place in the Palais de Chaillot, in the still spartan atmosphere of post-war Paris. On the ferry home, Arnold gave the manuscript of the full score to Ruth Railton's assistant. Like many another score from this period, that of Arnold's opus 24 cannot now be found. With the aid of the orchestral parts, sketches and a prodigious memory, he did, though, reconstruct and rewrite the Divertimento some years later.

Arnold's music continued to appear with some frequency on Ruth Railton's programmes, notably at the Edinburgh Festival in 1953, when his English Dances were heard north of the border for the first time, along with one of the earliest concert performances of the suite from Arnold's Coronation ballet, *Homage to the Queen*. Certainly his music proved to be well within the grasp of the young players; as did the Second Symphony when he rehearsed it with them himself much later, in 1956, at the end of a year in which he had also served on the Council of the NYO. Ruth Railton described Arnold, with some justification, as the NYO's 'more-or-less resident composer'[13] during its formative years.

In the late 1940s, Arnold was also becoming more ambitious. *Beckus the Dandipratt* had several successors, the *Festival Overture* written for his old teacher Philip Pfaff in 1946 and then in 1948 *The Smoke*, written for the Bournemouth Municipal Orchestra (as it was then called) and the conductor Rudolf Schwarz. 'The Smoke' was cockney slang for London and the piece is an extrovert, often jazzy, impression of metropolitan life. For the eminent clarinettist Frederick Thurston, always known as Jack, Arnold wrote the first in what was to prove a long line of concertos for friends in the musical profession.[14]

Malcolm Arnold has observed more than once that in his concertos, he usually wrote with the sound and artistry of a particular soloist in his mind's ear. The soloists often being close friends, he was able to tailor the writing to that artist's personality. There is, not surprisingly, less of a logical line of musical development in the concertos than in his symphonies, but he makes up for this with an enormous variety of musical character. Arnold was to number among his friends instrumentalists as diverse as the horn-player Dennis Brain, the flautist Richard Adeney, the clarinettist Benny Goodman and Larry Adler the harmonica virtuoso – among others. Their personalities are clearly audible in their concertos, yet the Arnold imprint is not lacking either. So, in the First Clarinet Concerto, there was plenty for Jack Thurston to relish. As a player of noted rhythmic precision he enjoyed the preponderance of off-beat entries in the first movement and the rhythmic hiccoughs in the second subject, written in alternating bars of four and three crotchets. Similarly the finale, headed allegro con fuoco and written in six-eight metre, is full of an almost wild energy. As for outward and visible indications of the Concerto's composer, there is a forward momentum increasingly to be found in these early works that is often counterbalanced by passages of apparent stasis or instability. At times in this Concerto, the soloist is silent for long periods and the strings assume the foreground, most conspicuously so at the end of the slow movement, where the writing is sombre and almost edgy, reminiscent of parts of Benjamin Britten's *Les Illuminations* written only eight years previously. Rehearsing the piece, Jack Thurston suggested that Arnold should fill in some of these holes and the composer agreed without hesitation. The additions were written directly into the clarinet part, and the full score, at the rehearsal. Curiously, the Second Clarinet Concerto, written in 1977 for Benny Goodman, has distinct similarities to its predecessor in the harmonic ambiguities and uncertainties of its central lento movement. These only go so far, however; unlike the work for Jack Thurston, Benny Goodman's Concerto ends with a hysterical squib called 'The Pre-Goodman Rag'.

Hardly surprisingly, with all this compositional activity, tension was beginning to build up between the creative and performing sides of Malcolm Arnold's preoccupations. Even though the LPO was generous in allowing him time away from orchestral duties, it was becoming obvious by 1948 that the situation would soon need to be resolved one way or another. Matters were taken out of his hands by the award to him of the Mendelssohn Scholarship by the Royal College.

The honour was a considerable one. At the time, the prize was the most valuable of its kind in Britain. In addition, the connection with Mendelssohn was no mere caprice: the prize had been created by the composer's friends in Leipzig after his death, with the original intention of enabling musicians to study at the Leipzig Conservatoire. Their appeal for funds had found ready support in England, where Mendelssohn had conducted on several occasions, and eventually an independent British fund was established, after a highly successful benefit performance of *Elijah*. Sullivan was the first scholar in 1856 and others who preceded Arnold included Eugen d'Albert, Maud Valerie White and George Dyson, who was not only the Principal of the Royal College of Music but a member of the panel which awarded him the Mendelssohn Scholarship.

It was essentially a travelling bursary awarded to young composers to enable them to go abroad and widen their musical education. It prompted Arnold to make his definitive break with orchestral playing and convinced him that he should try his luck as a full-time professional composer. He took the advice of Sir George Dyson and went for several months to Italy, not for further study, but to shake himself free of London concert life and to listen to what music he could find.

In retrospect, his spell in Rome was a critical phase in Arnold's career. This was emphatically not because the scholarship gave him time off in which to compose. On his own admission he did not compose seriously at all. None the less he came back a composer, having set off for Italy as a trumpeter who composed. Above all, Italy gave him time to think and to be himself. He was for once able to listen to music objectively and he found plenty of opportunities to do so, at the opera and at concerts. One surprise was the prevailing high standards at the post-war Rome Opera House; Arnold admitted that it took him a little time to work out why. Quite simply, he was unfamiliar with the reputation of Tullio Serafin as a conductor. As for concerts, there were in particular weekly recitals at the American Embassy where the seats were free. Here he met and enjoyed the company of Alexei Haieff, a Russian-born composer who had managed to leave Stalin's Russia for the United States in his teens, had then been a pupil of Nadia Boulanger in Paris and was now teaching at the American Academy in the Italian capital. Haieff, some seven years Arnold's senior, was an enthusiast for Stravinsky and for jazz and shared both passions with the Englishman.

There was one project on which Arnold did work intermittently in the Italian sunshine: an opera. Through his earliest work at the Denham film studios the previous year,[15] he had got to know one of the scriptwriters, Joseph Henry Mendoza. For a period of some years Arnold and Joe Mendoza were on close terms and the composer even wrote a short choral piece, Two Ceremonial Psalms, for the wedding in 1952 at the Marble Arch synagogue of his friend's sister, Anne Mendoza. He set Psalm 95 and Psalm 100, for unaccompanied sopranos and altos. Writer and composer were to work on two operatic projects: the first of them, *Henri Christophe*, based on the life of the first black ruler of Haiti, was immensely ambitious in conception and was intended as an entry in the Festival of Britain opera competition. The project eventually foundered when the assessors were not sufficiently impressed to give a grant towards its completion.

After his return from Italy, Arnold did not abandon the trumpet totally; the process was a gradual one. He still accepted engagements with *ad hoc* ensembles such as Karl Haas's London Baroque Ensemble, where he happily encountered once again the horn-player Dennis Brain. One of their appearances together, and one of Arnold's last as an instrumentalist, was at a series of open-air concerts in Russell Square. In the course of it a Cherubini march reduced the players to near-hysteria when the prevailing wind played havoc with the music on the stands, causing them to lose count of the repeats. The march apparently threatened to go on for ever, until the wind finally came to the rescue by blowing the music away altogether.

He also resumed contact with other friends outside music. Through Constant Lambert, the young Arnold also rubbed shoulders occasionally with an altogether different set. Lambert had links with a tight-knit circle at the BBC, mostly associated with the fledgeling Third Programme, established in 1946 from a mixture of high cultural purpose and post-war euphoria. As a result, in Lambert's wake he would find himself from time to time drinking in the pubs and clubs around Broadcasting House. Those he met were the creative spirits behind the Features Department, then the jewel in the radio crown. They included figures such as Louis MacNeice and Laurence Gilliam, David Lloyd James, and Val Gielgud, who was in charge of drama. Another composer, Elisabeth Lutyens, was sometimes darkly visible in a corner of The George on Great Portland Street. He missed seeing Dylan Thomas, by now famous and busy across the Atlantic. The artist Michael Ayrton was often part of the crowd, and their acquaintance was sealed when, later in the Fifties, both became members of the Savile Club in Brook Street. That institution became in time the focal part of Arnold's London existence when he had moved away from the capital. Less flamboyant than the Garrick, less intellectual than the Athenaeum, the Savile suited both the diversity of his interests and his love of stimulating company to the full.

The friendship with Constant Lambert reinforced yet another musical acquaintanceship which dated back to LPO days. Lambert was renowned as a fine narrator of *Façade*, that bizarre entertainment combining recitation and music devised by Walton and Edith Sitwell. Arnold too loved the outrageous side of *Façade*, the jazzy rhythms, popular tunes, virtuosic if often meaningless words, and exaggerated feeling of Twenties decadence; *Façade* gave him a kinship with both Lambert and William Walton, via the notion of the artist as Clown or Jester. The two composers saw one another often, and with enjoyment; as time went by, each was to influence the other's music. When Walton retreated to the Italian island of Ischia with his Argentinian wife Susanna, continuing contact remained a priority for them both.

Perhaps the fullest indication of the impact of his first visit to Italy on Arnold, and of the way his stay there clarified his ambitions, is the date at the end of his most important score to this date: his First Symphony, completed on 16 February 1949. By his own account he did not work at it while in Italy; it was therefore the fruit of intensive work during the autumn and winter of 1948. The Symphony was written not to a commission, but out of inner necessity, and the first performance did not take place for a further two and a half years, at the 1951 Cheltenham Festival. When it was heard, its importance was immediately recognised: 'In the First Symphony, he proved his ability to speak in the bold and plain terms appropriate to a big "public" work and to use his basic material consistently, cogently and economically, sticking firmly to the main issues. The tone of voice is objective; Arnold seems to be flexing his symphonic muscles, proving to the world and to himself that he is capable of great things.'[16]

Cheltenham was its logical destination. Under the twenty-five-year directorship of G. A. M. Wilkinson, the Cheltenham Festival had become the principal forum for British contemporary music and the term 'Cheltenham Symphony' still carried with it prestigious associations, as well as expectations of high craftsmanship. Later, towards the end of the Fifties, when the more radical attitudes of European modernism started to influence the British avant-garde, Cheltenham began to lose its reputation and even to become a term of derision – but not yet.

Arnold had in fact had two trial runs, with a Symphonic Suite, now lost, and a Symphony for Strings, op. 13, full of a Bartók-like astringency. The First Symphony turned out to be rich in originality and drama. It has an arresting start, its themes hammered out rapidly first on timpani and heavy brass, then by harsh unison woodwind, and the scoring brings to mind another work that the young composer had heard played and admired: Shostakovich's Fifth Symphony. Later in the first movement, we seem to be in the forlorn, desolate world of parts of Gustav Mahler's Second and Third Symphonies, which Eduard van Beinum had opened up to Arnold shortly before in concerts with the LPO. The comparison with Mahler is relevant in other ways too. The path of the music is not always governed by strict symphonic logic and the establishment of a particular mood or atmosphere can take precedence, as happens in the middle of the first movement when Arnold seems almost to lose his way, before matters are settled in the tormented resolution, with repeated brass fanfares and a tune in minims over another strong timpani pattern.

The other movements share this sense of unease. The slow movement matches broad solos for oboe and clarinet with more strident outbursts in clashing keys and further solos over an accompaniment that another growing Arnold hero, Hector Berlioz, would have been proud of: menacing repeated quavers on low brass, devoid of any harmonic momentum, with quiet strokes on the tam-tam. As for the finale, it plunges into headlong movement, with driving rhythms and often strident textures in the orchestra. Little seems to challenge the urgent opening theme. It is put through a variety of hoops and is even turned into a quick string fugue, until suddenly the music veers into a wholly unrelated key and Arnold writes a grotesque parody of a military march.

Is this bizarre march episode an echo of Arnold's bizarre wartime experiences? Or is it merely 'an artful use of chiaroscuro to enhance the contrasts in the picture'?[17] How true is it, by contrast, that at the end 'a long-breathed melody is at last permitted full rein to sing its anguished response to the follies of war'?[18] These are matters of opinion not fact and it is one of the enduring challenges of music that it is not possible to pin down its multiple meanings in words. Throughout his musical career Arnold has offered few verbal clues; he was happy to trust his musical instincts and his subconscious mind without recourse to words. The facts of the case are that soon after the Cheltenham performance of the First Symphony, he was at work on the Second Symphony, and that from then on the writing of symphonies was seldom far from his mind, even when there was no immediate prospect of performance. This compulsion was one reason why he was driven to become a composer and therefore to forsake his chosen instrument.

Back in the late Forties, there was another reason why he was able to make that break. A development was set in train that was to have profound repercussions on the rest of his career. In 1947 Malcolm Arnold wrote his first cinema score, for a short film called *Avalanche Patrol*, about the Swiss Mountain Rescue Service. By 1969, when he called a halt after *David Copperfield*, he had written the music for 116 films alone, not counting music for radio, television and the stage. It was more than enough – a chapter of his life that could constitute a book in itself.

3 : Rhapsody for Orchestra

or *The Sound Barrier*

'I'm lucky to be alive,
the way I had to work on that film!'

In the years after the Second World War a composer's life was not – as indeed it seldom is at any time – a financially happy one. Despite the occasional commission for concert music, Malcolm Arnold was initially only able to become a full-time composer by relying for his bread and butter on one particular source: the newly resurgent British film industry.

The suggestion that Arnold should send something of his own to the Denham film studios had actually come from a colleague in the LPO. Sidney Twinn was a string player whose name had first appeared among the second violins in 1942. Having experienced Arnold's work literally at first hand, he repeatedly pressed the composer to create an opening for himself in a medium they both appreciated. So Arnold sent off the score of *Beckus the Dandipratt*, and the die was cast. One advantage was that his publishers, Lengnick, had a fine copyist in their employ, Philip Godfrey Jones, whose work can still be seen in some of the Lengnick scores. The meticulous accuracy and clarity of the music as presented helped Arnold's cause considerably when it arrived on the desk of John Hollingsworth, the assistant music director at the Denham Studios. He had heard some of Arnold's other music and was enthusiastic. As a result, it was John Hollingsworth who in

1947 conducted the London Symphony Orchestra in *Avalanche Patrol*, the first film music Arnold wrote.

So began a very rapid apprenticeship that was to culminate, years later, in a string of distinguished scores such as *Whistle Down the Wind*, *The Inn of the Sixth Happiness* and *The Bridge on the River Kwai*, which won Arnold a Hollywood Oscar. His natural ability as a film composer catapulted him to fame and fortune and into rubbing shoulders with some of the great names of the cinema: Joseph Mankiewicz, Richard Attenborough, Bryan Forbes, John Huston, Carol Reed, David Lean, John Mills. Arnold's name became familiar to a whole generation of cinema-goers years before the wider concert-going public had a chance to take him seriously. The Fifties were the last golden flowering of British cinema before television took away the audiences and the money, and Malcolm Arnold was an integral part of that flowering. Ironically it is now television and the video industry that prevent Arnold's films from falling into total oblivion – and which to the envy of colleagues have kept his income flowing with regular repeats of some of the more famous films, reissues on video-cassette and even the occasional showing on satellite channels of something long forgotten.

If Arnold found that writing film music came easily to him this was in part – or so he claimed – the result of being a natural film fan. The apprenticeship was so fast that within a year he was working on his first feature film, *Badger's Green*, directed by John Irwin to a screenplay by the playwright R. C. Sherriff. Muir Matheson conducted the orchestra for the sound-track, as he was to do on innumerable future occasions. For the most part, though, Arnold learned his trade by writing music for all kinds of short documentaries. In 1948, for instance, when he worked on a dozen films in all, there were two short films for the Central Office of Information, *Report on Steel* and *Mining Review*. Other titles from the same year have a similar flavour: *Hydrography*, for instance, or *Cotton – Lancashire's Time for Adventure*. This last was made by a production company called This Modern Age, with whom Arnold and Matheson developed a regular and profitable association.

The course of Arnold's involvement in the film business was never likely to be entirely trouble-free, and he had an early illustration of this in 1949, over what was only his second feature film, *Britannia Mews*, based on a novel by Margery Sharp. Muir Matheson, who was to conduct the Royal Philharmonic at the sessions, and whose word was law at the studios, insisted on some changes to the score; with the result that, for a time, Arnold stuck to documentaries, where he enjoyed a greater musical freedom. Only his growing reputation in this field established an artistic authority sufficient for him to return to features on his own terms.

By the mid-Fifties Malcolm Arnold was in such demand for feature films that, with very few exceptions, documentary work was squeezed out altogether. Arnold was hugely gratified at the direct contact with the musically unsophisticated audience offered by the cinema; his success gave him a foothold into a different, grass-roots culture of a kind which few composers enjoy, and which reinforced his increasing belief in music's need to communicate directly with an audience. On the other hand he could also see, early on, that his own efforts in entirely other and more conventional spheres of musical activity would, unless he were careful, become progressively overshadowed. Rather than make a pact with the Devil and abandon art for Mammon, he began to lead a double life.

For nearly twenty years he maintained a prodigious output, in effect undertaking the work of two men, often by working far into the night. His own account of working on his most famous film score, *The Bridge on the River Kwai*, written in 1957, is not untypical of the kind of musical life he was now forced to lead: 'From the point of view of time, the music for *The Bridge on the River Kwai* was the worst job I ever had in my life. From the time of seeing the film to the time of recording the music, I had ten days to write about forty-five minutes' worth of music. One usually has longer than that.'[1]

Most of Arnold's other film scores were similarly written at breakneck speed and over the years the demands on his physical and mental stamina – and, according to John Amis,[2] on his family and friends – were enormous. Writing for the cinema refined Malcolm Arnold's composing technique to a pitch seldom granted to his contemporaries and gave him a fluency that others could only envy. The composer himself, however, denied that music came easily to him: 'I have a reputation for facility, for being able to write all sorts of music easily. Don't believe it. I have to get into an almost suicidal state before I get the manuscript paper out and start putting notes down.'[3]

Real or forced, Arnold's fluency was rivalled only by other precocious musicians such as André Previn, who started in Hollywood even younger. At the same time, though, writing for the screen laid Arnold's more serious compositional efforts open to the damaging charges of facility and superficiality, charges which the critics did not hesitate to make, even as friendly a voice as Donald Mitchell: 'In Arnold's case I suspect that fertility and facility go hand in hand.'[4]

Despite the dangers and stresses, there is no doubt that Arnold found working in films a huge and stimulating challenge. He knew the importance of the score in achieving the film's effect on its audience. That was why the composer normally had a separate screen credit, even if studios and directors sometimes treated him with incomprehension and disdain. At other times, they would turn to him in desperation. 'A composer is always being asked to rescue films, or at least parts of them. Film-makers expect this of composers. The American film-director Adolf Deutsch said, "A musician is like a mortician. He can't bring a body to life, but he can make it look better!"'[5]

The film titles for which Arnold wrote the music reveal the extraordinarily wide subject-matter which he had to embrace. At one extreme there were patriotic newsreels such as *This is Britain* (1950) or *The Royal Tour – New Zealand* (1954). There was a solid wedge of war-films, including – in 1969, when he had already decided to give up writing for films – *Battle of Britain*, which he took over from William Walton when his friend got stuck part-way through. At the other extreme there were the famous St Trinian's films, farcical schoolgirl romps directed by Sidney Gilliat and Frank Launder which were enormously popular in their time. The sequence began with the Belles of that unique educational establishment and ended with a score for *The Great St Trinian's Train Robbery* (1966). Even after that, yet another St Trinian's film used sections from previous scores after Arnold declined to write a fresh one. For the very first of them, he even had to write a 'St Trinian's School Song'![6]

Film music seldom stands up to scrutiny away from the context for which it was provided, though Malcolm Arnold's music is often an exception and in one or two cases he deliberately fostered the process. These were exceptions, however, and he knew it. *The Bridge on the River Kwai* won its Oscar not for its original melodic material alone but for the originality of treatment of the musical element within the context of Pierre Boulle's story. Most famously, in the camp scene Arnold combined the familiar March 'Colonel Bogey' with an ingenious counter-melody of his own, in the process running into copyright difficulties with the estate of the march's original composer, Kenneth Alford.

All this was on top of the sheer technical difficulties of making the music fit the picture. Arnold himself liked to quote one example: 'The sequence when the soldiers first arrive at the camp was quite difficult to record. I had seventeen members of the Irish Guards and a piccolo player whistling, and they had to march in sand to get the sound of the footsteps. I recorded the orchestra afterwards. It was quite complicated.'[7]

The quarrying of familiar material was a trick to which he was not afraid to have regular recourse. For *Tunes of Glory*, directed in 1960 by Ronald Neame and starring John Mills in the role he nominated as his favourite, Arnold found a winning number in a traditional Scottish tune, 'The Black Bear'. In his slightly jazzy arrangement, with trombones prominent, it captured exactly the right note of nonchalant military heroism. A year later, for Bryan Forbes's *Whistle Down the Wind*, he incorporated contributions from a successful pop group, The Spinners, adjusting with ease to their style and idiom.

Other assignments demanded even greater adjustments. For *Island in the Sun* (1957) Arnold briefly studied West Indian music on the island of Grenada as a preparation for writing his own score. Five years later he went even further afield. A feature film based on the life of Mahatma Gandhi, *Nine Hours to Rama*, was produced and directed in 1962 for Twentieth Century Fox by Mark Robson and was largely set in India. The story was taken up with the assassination of the Mahatma in January 1948. Arnold decided that the musical matter therefore had to be largely Indian and his score represents a considerable feat of assimilation. In preparation, he visited India and absorbed in a very short time much of the characteristic feeling and techniques of the sub-continent's music, as well as the instrumental possibilities and techniques it offered. To the true *aficionado* of classical Indian ragas the result may sound like an heretical pastiche; in the cinema the result sounds neither patronising nor offensive, but on the contrary buttresses the film's considerable tension admirably. There are other moments where the Arnold of the concert hall surfaces without embarrassment – the 'Malabar Hill' section might almost find a place in the slow movement of an Arnold Flute Concerto, such is the languorous charm of the flute solo.

Otherwise there was only a minimal amount of conscious overlap between the two halves of Malcolm Arnold's composing activity at this period. In 1949, for Anglo-Scottish Films, he provided the music for *The Beautiful County of Ayr* and based his score on tunes written by the Ayrshire poet Robbie Burns. One of those Burns tunes found its way, eight years later, into the first of the exhilarating Four Scottish Dances, op. 59. In 1951 he used a theme from his music for *Report on Steel* as the basis for the variations that make up a concert work, the Symphonic Study: *Machines*, op. 30, which lay unperformed for another thirty years. The title, and indeed some of the music, is reminiscent of another notorious pre-war factory piece, Alexander Mossolov's *Symphony of Machines*, full of post-1917 euphoria and the white heat of the Soviet technological revolution. The abrupt contrasts in Arnold's fourth variation are the audible counterpart of intercut shots in the film. Eventually Arnold's musical machine grinds to a halt by ramming home the key of C major with all the force of a steam piston.

Another attempt at crossing the boundary between screen and

concert hall brought greater success, including release on one of the next gramophone records of his music to be made after *Beckus the Dandipratt*. The first of his films for David Lean was *The Sound Barrier* (1952), to a screenplay by Terence Rattigan. Lean had assembled a star-studded cast including Ralph Richardson, Ann Todd, Denholm Elliott, John Justin and Dinah Sheridan, and the film was clearly destined from the outset for a high profile. Supersonic flight was a matter of widespread public fascination at this period. The film eventually included some aerial sequences that for their time were of breathtaking immediacy, involving longer than usual musical passages, free of dialogue. One section in particular involved what amounted to an aeroplane ballet, poetry in flight high in the skies. So effectively does the score reflect the notion of remoteness from earth – Arnold used a threesome of the highest instrument in the orchestra, the piccolo – that even away from the screen the vapour trails still seem visible to the mind's eye.

Confident of the success of David Lean's film even before the première, in May 1952 Arnold condensed his twenty-six minutes of music into a ten-minute concert piece – to which he added the title Rhapsody, op. 38, as an escape clause. As a reminder of the film it could not but work; as a self-contained concert work originating from such a source, though, it stood open to the charge of lacking logical coherence and sure enough some critics claimed that the *Sound Barrier* Rhapsody had some trouble taking off.

If it is true that the most effective parts of *The Sound Barrier* film score are those which are synchronised precisely to the visual image, how was this achieved? Working to split-second timings and the stop-watch might be thought unduly restrictive. Malcolm Arnold found otherwise.

> The most difficult problem in music is form, and in a film, you already have this solved for you. You have a blueprint, as it were, of the basic structure. I compare writing for the films to solving jigsaw puzzles. Sometimes it is difficult, but this stimulates me all the more, especially when I have to work things out to seconds, or fractions of them. I used to work with a stop-watch, but I now find there are basic tempos of music one gets to know so well that one

> can synchronise without a watch. If a film has been well cut, the various sequences will suggest their own rhythms and tempos. Sometimes you feel the rhythm of a sequence is sagging, and you need to speed the tempo of the music a little to bring the rhythm back to life. A crude example would be a chase sequence in which the cars don't seem to be going as fast as they should. A composer could very easily create the necessary additional excitement with the music.[8]

In his concert music Malcolm Arnold largely kept such direct emotional manipulation at bay, even if his detractors have occasionally cried foul: there is always the lure of the big tune, the final maestoso statement, as for instance at the end of the Second Symphony, op. 40. Usually there is musical logic on Arnold's side. Every case is different: in a much later work, the Second String Quartet of 1975, the golden glow of the slow tune that makes up its final pages acts like balm after the unbridled tonal conflicts that have run through the entire quartet; while in the Fifth Symphony of 1961 the whole convention is stood on its head, to shattering effect, when the return of the big tune from the slow movement at the very end of the whole Symphony is undermined by the bleak chords of A minor which follow it. One could see this return of the slow theme as equivalent to Hollywood's instinct for a happy ending – an instinct, however natural, doomed here to frustration. And there is another intriguing gloss to be put on Arnold's intentions. 'What Arnold is rejecting here is not hope, but *false* hope; not consolation, but *cheap* consolation.'[9]

The Hollywood cliché is thus given a revivifying twist in Arnold's concert music. Most of his works, whether on screen or concert platform, establish their own area of musical truth, to which he is invariably loyal.

His film output during the 1950s was prodigious. In 1958 the *Evening Standard* estimated Arnold's income as £10,000 per year. The figure could have been inaccurate by as much as half and would still have represented substantial wealth. Another sum quoted in the newspapers was an estimate of what each film was worth: £1500 at least. During the decade he was involved in some sixty-five films, of every conceivable kind, of which the following are only the most famous:[10]

1951 *No Highway*
1952 *The Sound Barrier*; *It Started in Paradise*
1953 *Albert RN*; *Hobson's Choice*
1954 *The Belles of St Trinian's*; *The Sea Shall Not Have Them*
1955 *I am a Camera*; *The Deep Blue Sea*; *1984*
1956 *Tiger in the Smoke*
1957 *Island in the Sun*; *The Bridge on the River Kwai*; *Dunkirk*
1958 *The Key*; *The Roots of Heaven*; *The Inn of the Sixth Happiness*
1959 *Suddenly Last Summer*

Every film presented a different set of problems; there seemed to be as many different demands made of the composer as there were directors and as many different solutions required as well. One thing Arnold rapidly acquired was confidence in his own judgements. In 1951, for instance, he told Henry Koster, the director of *No Highway*, that music was unnecessary in the film. 'I said if you're going to have music here, you're going to ruin a good script and a good film. What you need is title music, and that's all I will write.'[11] As a result, his name did not appear on the film's credits.

There were, inevitably, other occasional upsets. In 1956 he wrote the music for a remake of *The Barretts of Wimpole Street*, but it was rejected by the producers as not good enough. In the grip of depression in 1959 he was unable to complete the score of *Suddenly Last Summer* and another composer, Buxton Orr, finished it. Curiously, that same year Arnold had himself helped out a stranded producer, King Vidor, when he urgently wanted a replacement score for *Solomon and Sheba*. Producers, as much as the subject-matter, often influenced musical decisions: by command of the studios *Solomon and Sheba* was written for just ten musicians, *Whistle Down the Wind* for not many more, whilst Ralph Thomas wanted an impressively large orchestral sound for *No Love for Johnnie* and encouraged Arnold to write the title sequence for brass band.

Among all Arnold's numerous collaborations in the cinema, one in particular stands out. Not for nothing was Arnold sometimes sardonically referred to by colleagues as 'Master of the Lean's Music'. The success of *The Sound Barrier*, where the composer had shown a profound understanding of the director's intentions and realised them in his music, was followed in 1953 by David Lean's own screen adaptation of a famous stage play, *Hobson's Choice* by Harold Brighouse. The film starred Charles Laughton in the role of Henry Hobson, boot-maker, Brenda de Banzie as his strong-minded daughter and John Mills as Willie Mossop, the craftsman who is transformed by Maggie's love. Arnold's score found plenty of room for subtle nuance in what looked on the surface like a domestic drama with little room for manoeuvre: a self-important, brassy theme for the domineering Laughton character, a sequence showing the inside of Hobson's shop and the various items of footwear on display which preceded Hobson's drunken return home, an ambiguous Wedding-Night sequence and a triumphant apotheosis, love-theme prominent, as Willie takes over his father-in-law's business. Yet Arnold was restricted to the use of a fairly small orchestra of about twenty-five musicians. As a further constraint his music had to be added to the already finished film. So, for instance, the Shoe-Ballet music had to be tailored to fit the intricate visual sequence which David Lean had devised for the interior of Hobson's shop. The music was too good to disappear along with the film; but unwilling to repeat his earlier exercise with *The Sound Barrier* Malcolm Arnold showed little interest in recycling it. Only forty years later did another composer, Christopher Palmer, go to considerable lengths to construct elegant concert suites from this and a number of other long-buried film scores, in some cases reconstituting the music from the sound-track alone.

The third film of the Lean–Arnold trilogy was the familiar *The Bridge on the River Kwai*. For all the acclaim the film as a whole and Arnold's score in particular have never ceased to enjoy, there is no doubt that it left scars on him. The intense pressure generated by the unbelievable deadlines – at short notice Sam Spiegel wanted to send the film in for the Royal Command performance – was an extreme illustration of the principal factor contributing, eventually, to Arnold's decision to quit films altogether. Perhaps the best commentary on *Kwai* came from David Lean himself who, apart from muttering something about gongs, had left the composer entirely to his own devices. Writing from New York early in 1958 his assessment of Arnold's skill was precisely and gratefully expressed.

> I thought your score was simply *brilliant*. It gave me a hell of a kick when I heard it for the first time in the Columbia projection room here. I was in a dreadful state of dither, as you can imagine, but each time you came in and took over the thing with your music, I sat back in admiration, not only of you, but of my own work! God, what a gift you have, dear Malcolm. What *size*. What *sensitivity*. What *guts*. You didn't miss a bloody point – and the way you sneak in the march theme when old Nicholson wins and starts to do up that button on his tunic is sort of miraculous and fills me with a sort of wonder in the same way as I had it at your Coronation ballet. What an eye you have, coupled to that talent of yours! A dramatic eye, too. You know all the rules (by instinct I'm sure) of a good story teller. The way the music builds up from the above-mentioned moment – all sorts of undercurrents, question marks, suppressed excitements – and then – *boom!* – out it all spills, falling over itself, fulfilling itself, building and building and laughing and proud and crying and as unpompous as Punch! Tears started to my eyes and I too was as proud as Punch as the parade ground dust blew across the screen and the cheering men. I think it's the only moment I have ever really thought – looking at my own work – 'That is *really* good!' Sitting there I thought, 'How can I convey my thanks to him?' I wish I could.[12]

There are also some forty-five opus numbers – i.e. concert works – completed during the same period. The roots of the creative and physical crisis that was to afflict him in the late Seventies and Eighties are plainly evident here – in terms of sheer overwork. By the end of the Fifties Malcolm Arnold was carrying a workload which no artist under the sun could have sustained for as long as he did without crumbling under the strain.

4 : Philharmonic Concerto

or *Tunes of Glory*

'Music appeals to me chiefly because of its abstract quality . . .
for me the most worthwhile thoughts are to be expressed without words.'

Apart from the works that Malcolm Arnold did find time to compose in the Fifties there were several that he didn't. He told Roy Plomley in 1959[1] that he was working on a viola concerto for William Primrose – which makes at least one substantial project that never saw the light of day. In the course of the decade two further symphonies followed the Cheltenham première of the First Symphony and there were seven concertos, including works for his old friend the flautist Richard Adeney, the harmonica virtuoso Larry Adler, the oboist Léon Goossens, the horn-player Dennis Brain and the guitarist Julian Bream. He wrote innumerable shorter pieces, including a pair of Scottish-inspired masterpieces, the *Tam O'Shanter* Overture based on the famous Burns ballad, and four Scottish Dances which share much of the same spirit and end with a full-scale highland fling. *Tam O'Shanter*, incidentally, was not a sudden Burnsian flash-in-the-pan. Arnold had read all the volumes of Lockhart's monumental biography of the poet, as well as Lockhart's companion volumes on Walter Scott, during his youth in Northampton.[2] In Coronation Year, 1953, he wrote a full-length ballet for Covent Garden, *Homage to the Queen*, and subsequently two one-act ballets, *Rinaldo and Armida* and *Sweeney Todd*, both of which were also first performed by the Royal Ballet. This was also the decade of two of Arnold's operatic ventures and the start of his involvement with the musical circuses of Gerard Hoffnung. The chamber music includes the deeply-felt Piano Trio, op. 54. Before then, he published another set of children's pieces for piano in 1952 and occasionally dashed off music for his family to play at home in Richmond, Surrey. He wrote fanfares, a military march, a Toy Symphony and a Christmas Masque. Also dating from this period are two beautiful vocal works, the comparatively unfamiliar *John Clare* Cantata and the even less known solo settings of William Blake. In all this outpouring the musical standard is remarkably high. There is barely a single page, let alone a single work, which has not been carefully thought out and considered, without any loss of freshness or spontaneity. There were few interruptions to Arnold's labours. Perhaps the most affecting came in 1955 with the death of his mother on Malcolm Arnold's own birthday, 21 October, when the composer was thirty-four. Otherwise the pattern was one of relentless industry, much of it on behalf of friends.

'The gift of friendship' was Arnold's own memorable description of the function of his music: 'Music is a social act of communication, a gesture of friendship, the strongest there is.'[3]

Although film work consumed an enormous amount of his time and energy, financially it gave him greater freedom than that enjoyed by many another composer to write the concert music he chose, often for performers who were friends. Friendships from the Forties and even earlier remained strong and to them were added new ones. Of the earlier friends, he repaid his continuing debt to Philip Pfaff, his old teacher in Northampton, with a second piece, choral this time, which Pfaff conducted at its first outing. St Matthew's Church had acquired a new incumbent for whom the arts were a vital adjunct to worship and who was determined that his church would reflect the work of living artists as well as those of earlier generations. Walter Hussey was a remarkable organiser and fund-raiser, and gifted with the power of persuasion. Amongst those whom he commissioned during his time at Northampton were Henry Moore and Benjamin Britten;

later, when he became Dean of Chichester Cathedral, his scalps included Leonard Bernstein, John Piper and Marc Chagall. Aware of Arnold's growing reputation, and knowing of his connection with the town, Walter Hussey commissioned a setting of Psalm 150, *Laudate Dominum*, for the choir of St Matthew's, with organ accompaniment. For Arnold, 'it came at a time when I was very down. As a relief from film music, it was wonderful to get a commission.'[4] He set the Psalm in English, firmly in the mould of Anglican church music: the writing is simple and direct, mostly uncomplicated though with a few overlapping entries, several changes of tempo and key, and the hint of a dance tune in the organ part at the words 'Praise Him in the cymbals and dances'.

Friendships were also pursued through one of the lesser-known institutions of London musical life at this period. As well as of his favourite Savile Club, Arnold also became an *habitué*, along with many other musicians, of a remarkable organisation called the International Musicians' Association Club. John Amis was its secretary for a year in 1953. Its premises in South Audley Street offered not only out-of-hours hospitality in comfortable lounges and bars but a dining-room where, in Jack Brymer's phrase, 'you could get a meal equal to anything at the Ritz for a sixth of the price'.[5] Brymer also recalled seeing Arnold there regularly; and much later he took Arnold's Second Clarinet Concerto into his repertoire and became one of its most brilliant exponents. The explanation for the Club's existence lay in its support from a wealthy American lady named Mrs Hubbard whose admiration for British music and musicians led her to underwrite the Club's losses as a tax-deductible expense. She also saw it as a way of controlling her notoriously wayward musical son Tony. Sadly the taxman eventually objected and the Club closed, depriving Arnold of a much-loved haunt.

Among College friends, the link with Richard Adeney continued to bear musical fruit. After the Flute Sonatina, op. 19, came first an ingeniously economical Divertimento for wind trio, which Adeney performed with the oboist Sidney Sutcliffe and the clarinettist Stephen Waters who had played with Arnold in the

LPO. Its six short movements take less than ten minutes all told, but contain a wealth of melodic invention and ingenious contrasts. A full-scale Concerto for Flute and Strings followed in 1954 and turned out to be a real test of its dedicatee's virtuosity. Its first movement set Richard Adeney a whole range of problems, with scurrying semiquavers, maximum contrasts of staccato and legato, and bold demands for dynamic extremes: not usually the flute's forte. The middle movement is by contrast subdued, almost withdrawn, while the finale settles in G major, its hurtling pulse booby-trapped with the occasional irregular bar in a different metre. The friendship between the two men survived, though, and nearly twenty years later, in 1973, it even engendered a Second Flute Concerto, whose finale is this time a slow movement with a single haunting theme, full of wistful melancholy – which places an interesting light on the tribute Arnold paid at the time to his old acquaintance: 'To be asked by a performer whose accomplishment one admires so much is the greatest incentive to write music, and the style and the form of the piece are dictated by what I consider to be the main characteristics of Richard Adeney's great artistry.'[6]

Richard Adeney's own comment on their relationship during the Fifties and beyond, however, suggests that some of its early warmth had cooled, and that there were ominous shadows on the horizon: 'I was still friendly with Malcolm Arnold for many years, but later on his new malicious sense of humour frightened and hurt me. I could not keep up with his drinking, and was irritated by his linking drunkenness with prestige; so, although we still saw a lot of each other when working, we were no longer such close friends.'[7]

Nineteen fifty-one saw the start of another friendship which was destined to last for over forty years until Sir Charles Groves died in 1992. Though the conductor had not given the first performance of the composer's English Dances, op. 27, he was quick to programme them for a broadcast with the then BBC Northern Orchestra (now the BBC Philharmonic). The English Dances were the idea of Bernard de Nevers of Arnold's publisher Alfred Lengnick & Co. Suggesting to the composer the idea of a suite of dances based on English themes, he sowed the seed of what was to become a productive and profitable plant in Arnold's catalogue. He was duly rewarded with the dedication of the first set, though Arnold's melodies turned out to be wholly his own. The Dances are some of Arnold's most characteristic music of the early Fifties, boldly orchestrated in primary colours, extrovert in their rhythmic verve, full of memorable themes, which sometimes sound intentionally like folk melodies but are pure Arnold invention. (A second set of English Dances, completed the following year, represented Arnold's first appearance at the Henry Wood Proms in the Royal Albert Hall.) As it happened, though, the gratification felt by Bernard de Nevers was short-lived. Soon after the English Dances, there came a development that would be significant in the life of any creative artist. Arnold changed his publisher, moving from the firm of Alfred Lengnick to Paterson's Publications. The change bears certain marked similarities to Benjamin Britten's departure from Boosey & Hawkes in favour of Faber Music, a decade later. In each case, the composer in question moved to a firm that operated almost exclusively on his behalf. Paterson's came largely to revolve around Malcolm Arnold, and it was owned and managed by his friend Michael J. Diack, who was also an amateur horn-player of considerable skill. Arnold remained with Paterson's until well after the firm had ceased to manage his affairs with maximum efficiency, and his royalties may have diminished as a result. But he preferred to stay loyal to the firm he knew, rather than sacrifice a friendship on the altar of business efficiency.

The English Dances, though, belong firmly to Lengnick, who even commissioned another of their composers, Franz Reizenstein, to make a two-piano arrangement. Charles Groves took an immediate liking to the music and to its composer, and went on to become a loyal champion of Malcolm Arnold on the rostrum, giving several pieces by his friend their world première, including two of the symphonies.

The most notable of occasions from this period took place on 25 May 1953 – they met for the first time at the rehearsals – when Groves conducted the first performance of Arnold's

Second Symphony, op. 40, with the musicians whose Principal Conductor he had then become, the Bournemouth Municipal Orchestra. It had been commissioned by the Orchestra for its Diamond Jubilee, and the composer dedicated the new work to them – and to Charles Groves. On his appointment, Groves had boldly telephoned the composer he admired, introduced himself, and suggested he write a short piece for his new orchestra. He was somewhat shaken by the reply: 'Would you like the new symphony I'm writing?' But nothing ventured, nothing gained, and he accepted it sight unseen. The Second Symphony established Malcolm Arnold as an international force. Within a year it had been heard on the continent of Europe and in Canada; within three years it had been played in America and Africa; within ten years it had been played in Australia by the Sydney Symphony Orchestra. It was the first Arnold symphony to be recorded and it has seldom been out of the record catalogues for long. Even more than his First Symphony, the Second is the culmination of all Arnold's talent and musical experience to date, the years of studying, playing, listening, thinking, experimenting, writing for films, orchestras, chamber combinations of all shapes and sizes and finally of deciding for himself what sort of composer he wanted to be and what sort of music he wanted to write.

This much is apparent from the very first page. The individual voice behind the opening statements of this pastoral allegretto is clear in the remaining movements as well, despite strong echoes of Sibelius in the following scherzo-and-trio, and the presence of Gustav Mahler in the third slow movement: bird-calls on a lone piccolo, atmospherically static harmony, prominent harp and tubular bells, and a quiet solo trumpet fanfare. Charles Groves once wrote of this movement as 'an elegy of tragic power, superbly sustained';[8] which is exactly what, in his hands, it became. The finale by contrast is first cousin to the rumbustious English Dances; until the arrival of unexpected episodes, initially in the shape of a canon for the brass and then a brittle, even cynical, piccolo solo over slithery string harmonics, xylophone and oompah bass. Fierce tonal conflicts are then generated and are not resolved until the symphony ultimately lurches into the key of E flat major for the home straight.

Sir Charles Groves was to stand by Arnold through thick and thin, programming his music when he could (sometimes in the face of determined opposition from reluctant orchestral managements), persuading young musicians of its worth, protesting if he thought injustices were being done, visiting the composer during his long period of illness to reassure him he was not forgotten. One of his last links with Arnold was to be the première of the Ninth Symphony in Manchester some forty years on, in January 1992, which Groves conducted just a few months before his death.

Another close personal friend of Malcolm Arnold from the Fifties, Julian Bream, has documented their shared history with considerable frankness and wit.[9] Amongst other things, Arnold was important to Bream precisely because he represented some kind of anchor in the chaotic sea that was contemporary music in the Fifties and early Sixties.

> It was refreshing to be with a man who still wrote music in the old traditional style, albeit with originality and exemplary skill. He was very brave; he had tremendous conviction about himself and his music, so he never changed his style. . . . I always felt sure there was more to Malcolm than met the eye or greeted the ear.[10]

Arnold and Bream made music together, gossiped together, drank together, improvised jazz together – there is a wonderful photograph of the pair in the late Fifties: the guitarist grins happily, while Malcolm Arnold sits at his Goff clavichord smoking a cigarette as they strum their way through the latest popular American hit. Something of their camaraderie can be sensed in the music Arnold wrote for his friend. While the Guitar Concerto has never been out of the catalogues since the day it first appeared, it was not the first product of their friendship. Early in 1955 he completed a five-minute Serenade for guitar and strings for Bream to play with the local orchestra in Richmond-upon-Thames, of which Sheila Arnold was leader. It is a quiet and delicate miniature that creates an almost Mediterranean nocturnal spell, and the writing for the instrument is already both natural and atmospheric, employing the favourite guitar device of harmonics, for instance. Bream and Arnold spent many a late night exploring guitar techniques together.

Then, four years further into their friendship, came an unequivocal masterpiece. First performed by Julian Bream with the Melos Ensemble at the Festival founded by Benjamin Britten in Aldeburgh, Malcolm Arnold's Guitar Concerto, op. 67, is full of the imprint of its dedicatee's personality, as well as the composer's own hallmarks. As an example of the latter, there is the second subject of the formally regular opening movement: a tune that is one of Arnold's most outstanding inventions, perfectly suited to the guitar, sweetly melancholy in inflection, and once heard, never forgotten.

Most original of all, though, is the slow central movement, much the longest of the concerto, which takes the form of a homage to the French jazz guitarist and founder of the legendary Hot-Club de France, Django Reinhardt. He was something of a hero to both Arnold and Bream – not least for his love of jazzing the classics: he made a famous version in the Thirties of the Bach Double Violin Concerto. Arnold's homage begins in stillness, and soon transmutes into an unsentimental elegy the particular private language of the blues, with glissandi prominent, a bass line played pizzicato, and in a quicker section late in the movement, some familiar and conventional jazz syncopation. It is a haunting and evocative piece, tailor-made for Julian Bream. Arnold's concerto finales are sometimes knockabout affairs, but here, sensing the fragility of the spell established by the Reinhardt movement, Arnold respects the mood rather ingeniously. The finale turns out to be a minuet in rondo form, and its slightly stately gait does not preclude a gentle humour and lyricism in its treatment.

Although the Guitar Concerto is one of the most substantial of all Arnold's concertos, both in length and in musical substance, one should not overlook the unobtrusive skill of the orchestration, by which a small chamber orchestra of single woodwind bears the weight of the musical argument without ever sounding impoverished, or threatening to overwhelm the soloist. Given the richness of this concerto it is no surprise to discover that either side of it, the composer was working on three of his symphonies. Julian Bream gratefully took the concerto into his repertoire as a more than adequate companion piece to Joaquin Rodrigo's *Concierto de Aranjuez*, edited it for publication, has played it all over the world, and recorded it twice, once with Arnold himself conducting, once with Simon Rattle at the helm.

Nor was the concerto the end of the affair. Twelve years after it, in 1971, Julian Bream played for the first time a new Arnold work, the fruit of his interest, amounting almost to an obsession, in the late Sixties and later with the free form of the Fantasia. Admiring Elizabethan models such as those of Giles Farnaby or Orlando Gibbons, Arnold used the Fantasy as a vehicle for a number of pieces for unaccompanied instruments – among which the guitar now took its place. The Fantasy for guitar, op. 107, perhaps wears its heart rather less obviously on its sleeve than the concerto. Its seven linked sections are none the less superbly crafted for the skill of Julian Bream. The first is a Prelude dominated by a three-note ostinato of the interval of a fourth, falling then rising, over which appear a succession of sweeping, majestic chords; the second is a scherzo in six-eight time, with chords in groups of three below rapid repeated notes; then comes an Arietta with a typical Arnold three-four melody, marked pp and cantabile; while the fourth section is a brief but energetic Fughetta, interrupted by the fifth, another Arietta whose languor is broken in the middle by five sinister chords played 'tambura', that is, with the knuckle knocking against the body of the instrument. The penultimate section is a March where the guitar cleverly creates a snare-drum effect that highlights the syncopations in the tune above, before the Postlude takes us back to the music of the opening. Arnold's Fantasy for his friend Julian Bream, subtle and intimate music, is a connoisseur's piece, a tribute to the kind of friendship that goes below the surface and appreciates and exploits the friend's strengths and skills. Julian Bream in turn was to stick to his friend through thick and thin, enjoying their carefree sessions in the Fifties, watching his growing success in the Sixties, missing him when he emigrated to Ireland in the Seventies, despairing when troubles poured down on his head during the Eighties, but rejoicing when towards the end of that decade Malcolm Arnold finally emerged into some sort of security and stability.

Another musician who was close to Arnold at this time was the great oboist Léon Goossens. He gave the first performance of Arnold's Oboe Sonatina early in 1951 and was presented with a perfectly-crafted miniature designed to show off the soloist's graceful cantilena and his ability to throw off staccato passages with ease. The finale is a jig with some very difficult sections and Arnold paid Goossens a nice tribute by writing an alternative and easier solo part for lesser mortals to play.

The Sonatina proved to be merely an upbeat, though, to a more substantial work commissioned by the oboist, the Concerto for oboe and strings, op. 39, written the following year. Many of the same qualities are apparent on a larger scale. This time, Arnold catered for his eminent soloist via a winding chromatic lyricism, employing usually very narrow intervals and none too predictable in direction. The dominance of this style is reinforced by the unusual order of the movements: the middle movement is a driving dance with more than a hint of Gustav Holst about it, while the Concerto ends with a slow movement that has the classical form of the minuet as its background.

Léon Goossens was delighted enough with the Concerto to order more of the same. In due course, three years later, he received the Quartet for oboe and strings, op. 61. Again it is a largely untroubled piece, with the seamless rise and fall of Goossens's incomparable line and phrasing evidently uppermost in the composer's mind. This time the rondo finale has a distinct kinship with a Viennese waltz! It is not surprising to discover that Arnold originally thought of calling this latest oboe work a Serenade.

Away from the essentially private world of chamber music, Malcolm Arnold was increasingly in the public eye. An episode of which he remained inordinately proud was the result of an invitation to a party at the Indian High Commission. In conversation with the High Commissioner, Krishna Menon (later to become a prominent Indian Defence Minister), Arnold learned that the recently adopted national anthem of the country, with tune and words by Rabindranath Tagore, did not exist in orchestral or band guise. Though it had been published as far back as 1912 and had been long associated with the Indian struggle for independence, the Constitutional Assembly only adopted it officially on 26 January 1950, two days before India was proclaimed a Republic. Arnold immediately volunteered to fill the gap and his offer was gratefully accepted.

After his auspicious Proms début with the second set of English Dances in 1952, Arnold kept up his run of appearances at the Royal Albert Hall with two concertos in successive years. In 1953 Paul Hamburger and Helen Pike were the soloists in a work for the infrequent combination of piano duet (four hands at one keyboard rather than two pianos) and strings. The slow movement is the most complex of the three and is a further example of Malcolm Arnold's preoccupation, round about the time of the First Symphony, with another classical form, the passacaglia – which does not stop him introducing a suspicion of jazz into the final variation! The finale too is full of lively syncopations set against a waltz motif. Paul Hamburger, one half of the duo team at the première, approved: 'During rehearsals there were only minimal changes. Though Malcolm is no pianist, the piano writing is extremely good, consisting mainly of schematic scales and chords, kept interesting by Malcolm's ingenuity with simple materials. In places (Finale) it is quite difficult to play, but never written against the instrument.'[11]

With his single soloist at the Proms the next year, the composer was less fortunate, though Larry Adler was to remain a firm admirer and friend. The American virtuoso, domiciled in England as a result of the McCarthyite witch-hunts in the United States, was a ubiquitous figure in British musical life at this time and the notion of a concerto for the instrument commissioned from a composer known for his ability to bridge gaps and cross brows appealed to the BBC. Adler himself, however, nearly wrecked the première, as he later admitted. Naturally enough he was happy to demonstrate to Arnold the strengths and weaknesses of his instrument beforehand, and he was full of praise for the resulting example of Arnold's ingenuity in writing for unlikely combinations. Seemingly from a combination of laziness and fear, Larry Adler did not begin to practise his Concerto until a fortnight before the first performance – disastrously late for someone who found learning by ear much easier than learning from the score. The resulting première, with the composer conducting the BBC Symphony Orchestra, was surprisingly well received; but both men knew that Adler's performance 'sounded, especially in the last movement with all the pyrotechnics and syncopation that Arnold had written, as if I hadn't learned it at all'.[12]

Characteristically, Arnold's Harmonica Concerto, op. 46, refuses to sound patronising. Despite its brevity – it lasts less than ten minutes – it is a significant contribution to the literature of this instrumental Cinderella. The challenge is tackled head on, for the orchestra includes not only strings, but four horns, three trumpets, three trombones, tuba, timpani and percussion. To make the point even clearer, the strings are silent in the slow movement, which results in textures of uncommon originality, as the harmonica enjoys its interplay with the heavy brass. And throughout, the limited technique of the mouth-organ is exploited with total sympathy, in rapid runs, glissandi and close-harmony chords. Virtuosos of the mouth-organ are not thick on the ground, but apart from Larry Adler, the Canadian Tommy Reilly also became a successful exponent of the concerto, recording it more than once.

Another friend, this time of long standing, made what turned out to be a final gesture of friendship in Malcolm Arnold's direction shortly before his tragic death. At the Tenth Aldeburgh Festival in 1957, Dennis Brain appeared in the Jubilee Hall not only as soloist in concertos by Haydn and Telemann, but also conducting the Dennis Brain Chamber Orchestra, with Hugh Bean leading what was evidently an *ad hoc* group of players. Rubbing shoulders with Mozart and Stravinsky alongside the two concertos were two contemporary pieces, one by Peter Racine Fricker, the other Malcolm Arnold's First Sinfonietta, then just three years old. The composer was present. Within three months, Dennis Brain was dead, his budding second career as a conductor barely begun. Arnold, almost paralysed with misery, was only able to exorcise his grief musically in what was to become his Fifth Symphony.

In the same Fifth Symphony, another close friend was also commemorated: Gerard Hoffnung. For a brief period in the Fifties, Hoffnung became Malcolm Arnold's regular partner in musical crime. Yet there was more to the relationship than meets the eye. Even though Hoffnung is primarily remembered today for his brilliant musical cartoons and the musical extravaganzas he organised at the Royal Festival Hall – Haydn's Surprise Symphony with the grandfather of all surprises, a Chopin mazurka played on four tubas, or the *Disconcerto*, a hilarious assembly by Franz Reizenstein of all the famous bits of other piano concertos, from Beethoven's 'Emperor' via Tchaikovsky to Rachmaninov's Second – Gerard Hoffnung had another, more serious side. He was a prison visitor, a Quaker, a member of the Howard League for Penal Reform, a compassionate and enlightened man who had the courage of his convictions, and was beginning to speak out at the time of his sadly early death. He died suddenly, at the age of thirty-four, of a cerebral haemorrhage, and Arnold was for a time bereft.

Part of Hoffnung's attractiveness lay in the fact that he was an outsider, the son of a family of German Jews who came to Britain when he was fourteen. This experience reinforced a natural anti-authoritarianism which resulted, early in his time in England, in expulsion from Hornsey College of Art – just as Arnold's sister Ruth had been banished from the Slade. Beneath the good-natured surface, the same subversive streak was present in much of Hoffnung's musical humour. He also loved, and was no mean exponent of, the tuba. This in turn may account for the unexpected melancholy of Malcolm Arnold's Fantasy for Tuba, written just a few years after Gerard Hoffnung's death. Their partnership, in the war against all forms of musical pomposity, was all too short.

Arnold's own contributions to the Hoffnung musical extravaganzas regularly verged on the surreal. The critic William Mann once described him in *The Times* as 'the nearest lunatic creative artist to Gerard that could be imagined without actually being Hoffnung'. It all began in 1956, when Hoffnung took over the Royal Festival Hall in London for what was billed as the Hoffnung Music Festival. In German, 'Hoffnung' means hope – something Gerard lived in continually. On the basis of only a slight acquaintance, but aware of his reputation as a composer with a rare sense of humour, Hoffnung commissioned Arnold to write an opener for the concert. The resulting work was to become one of music's most celebrated *jeux d'esprit* ever.

The Grand Grand Overture, dignified as opus 57, is scored for full orchestra, organ, three vacuum cleaners, one floor polisher, and four rifles. Complete with a coy programme note from Messrs Hoover, it duly brought the house down in the Royal Festival Hall. The audience that night seized gleefully on all the more obvious japes – not only the climactic silencing of the carpet-sucking wind-machines by the resident execution squad, but the many horrendous juxtapositions of key and the glorious apotheosis at the end, which is suitably debunked when the composer seems as if he is never going to bring it to an end! Yet hidden in the riot is also one of Malcolm Arnold's most memorable melodies ever, one which he might have justifiably held back for a 'proper' overture or symphony. But, generous to a fault, the thought never crossed his mind.

The Hoffnung Concert on 13 November 1956, which included the Grand Grand Overture, was to cement still further another long-standing friendship. Arnold was already at work on his new Horn Concerto, for Dennis Brain, and in the course of their association he had discovered that his distinguished horn-playing acquaintance had a second string to his bow, as it were. Dennis Brain was a competent organist, and the overture duly included an all-important organ part. It was a feature of the Hoffnung concerts, in their mad perversity, that famous soloists should depart in this way from their accustomed roles. Sure enough, on the same evening, Dennis Brain famously played a concerto by Leopold Mozart on a length of garden hosepipe. Stephen Pettitt comments that the result was 'a practical demonstration of

Dennis's insistence that the sound a horn-player produced was first and foremost the product of the physical make-up of the player himself'.[13] It was also an inadvertent example of Arnold's principle that a concerto should be tailored to the sound and style of its dedicatee – a principle that he was even then attempting to observe, in the work which he was to resume the following day: the new Horn Concerto for Dennis Brain.

The Hoffnung concerts have long passed into legend, and those who had the good fortune to be present had the advantage of enjoying the essential visual element which later generations, dependent on the records which have seldom been out of the catalogues, have necessarily had to do without. John Amis, a close friend of both Hoffnung and Arnold, has left an unforgettable memoir of Gerard Hoffnung that seeks to conceal neither the fact that he could sometimes be difficult to accommodate, nor the risks he was running. And Amis's descriptions of the preparations for the first of the Hoffnung concerts contains a tribute to Arnold as well.

> Perhaps the most thrilling moment of all was not the first concert itself, but the first rehearsal, with the Morley Orchestra, of the big commissioned piece for the first concert, Malcolm Arnold's Grand Grand Overture . . . That first rehearsal saw the unveiling of Malcolm's funny overture with that marvellous lyrical tune, slightly ironical of course, but so emotional that we were all caught up in a surge of joy and tears. It is one thing to write a symphony, but another matter entirely to write a great tune, a gift that should be cherished, but is all too often sneered at, these days.[14]

John Amis's wife, the violinist Olive Zorian, 'played' one of the parts for vacuum cleaner; the others, and the floor polisher, were taken by Hoffnung's wife Annetta, Pauline del Mar, married to the conductor Norman del Mar, and Jean Stewart, a viola player who had been the dedicatee of Vaughan Williams's string quartet! Writing of Arnold's early music years later, Amis finds in places 'a certain curiously urban loneliness'.[15] For him, this streak is all of a piece with the contradictory nature of the man himself. He points to the composer's manic highs after long periods under extreme pressure working on film scores, usually followed by periods of severe depression. 'His life became a see-saw. It was pathetic to witness, and it all but destroyed him.' Even in the Fifties, when his musical friendships were at their most intense, like most great clowns, including Gerard Hoffnung, Arnold was not immune.

Of course, there were people who saw this and indeed the whole Hoffnung exercise as an act of wanton desecration on some fine music. Gerard Hoffnung's response was to ask for more of the same. Two years later, at the 1958 Hoffnung Interplanetary Music Festival, Arnold produced a work that, as with the earlier Grand Grand Overture, contained some decent music as well as the obligatory comic ingredient: his United Nations.

The element of sharp satire is obvious enough in its baleful juxtaposing of various national anthems and marches; and when the same William Mann, quoted earlier, described the United Nations in his *Times* review of the concert as 'ultimately a document of hopeful internationalism', he was erring on the side of optimism. The scoring is for full orchestra, organ and 'as many military bands as there are entrances to the concert hall'. After a great many moments of musical near-anarchy more than reminiscent of the great American pioneer of such heterophony, Charles Ives, with national anthems frequently superimposed and fragments of familiar Tchaikovsky thrown in for good measure too, the conclusion is unexpectedly quiet. Whether this really does represent political harmony after the lusty satire that has come earlier is a moot point.

And then on 25 September 1959 came Hoffnung's death from leukaemia. It was entirely in the spirit of Hoffnung's life and personality that his friends and supporters should, for a few years at least, refuse to let the tradition of the Hoffnung Festivals merely wither away. For the Memorial Concert held in the Royal Festival Hall in October 1960, Arnold contributed a Hoffnung Fanfare for no fewer than thirty-six trumpets, and some extra animals for Saint-Saëns's celebrated Carnival – the Giraffe was followed by Sheep, Cows, Mice, Jumbo and finally Chiroptera – Bats – who needless to say are frantically active, but inaudible: the orchestra is totally silent at this point.

A year later, at the Hoffnung Astronautical Musical Festival,

Arnold bowed out with another two contributions. The first was a bizarre homage to Beethoven, mercilessly seizing on his famous indecision over the appropriate overture to his opera *Fidelio*. At the stage when it was still called *Leonora*, Beethoven wrote three successive versions. The audience in November 1961 were regaled with a fourth, which combined the merits and defects of its predecessors into one not always harmonious whole. The other Arnold work in the concert even merited an opus number! Opus 76 bears a French title: *Grand Concerto Gastronomique*. Scored, if that is the word, 'for eater, waiter, food and large orchestra,' it required the actors Henry Sherek and Tutte Lemkow to enact the ritual of a six-course meal to an appropriate musical accompaniment. Some idea of the proceedings may be gained from the programme-book:

I *Prologue*: Maestoso; *Oysters*: Moderato – Vivace
II *Soup, Brown Windsor*: Maestoso – Allegro vivace
III *Roast Beef*: Nobilmente
IV *Cheese*: Maestoso
V *Peach Melba*: Moderato e molto espressivo
VI *Coffee, Brandy, Epilogue*: Allegro moderato

Once again, the critic William Mann was there relishing every last morsel. While his tongue was still in his cheek he pointed out that, though the piece was unlikely to come over effectively on the gramophone, 'every greedyguts present enjoyed it enormously'.

The spirit of Gerard Hoffnung refused to die down, and his widow Annetta, to whom Arnold was very close for a time after Gerard's death, keeps the concerts alive to this day. Pieces such as the Grand Grand Overture or Leonora no. 4 still receive occasional airings in unlikely parts of the globe, where unsuspecting audiences must surely speculate on the integrity and motives of both perpetrator and composer, and shake their heads ruefully over these further convincing manifestations of the incomprehensible English character. As for Arnold's own musical sense of humour, there were to be countless further examples. Two concerto finales stand out: in the Concerto for two Pianos (Three Hands) and the Second Clarinet Concerto, laughter is clearly intended. The same is true of parts of the famous Fantasy for Audience and Orchestra which was to set alight the audience at the Last Night of the Proms in 1970.

The humour could of course be less broad, as in a gentle little piece written while Gerard Hoffnung was still alive. It was entirely characteristic of Arnold that another of his most light-hearted and immediately appealing works should be inscribed 'To the Musicians' Benevolent Fund', and that all his royalties should be made over to that body. A work for the young in heart thus helped the aged; nor is it a throwaway piece, for it carries an opus number and contains in its outer movement a pair of fine Arnold tunes. The instrumentation of Arnold's Toy Symphony, op. 62, demands to be quoted.

Quail
Cuckoo (doubling Guard's whistle)
Whistle in C sharp minor (doubling nightingale)
Trumpet in F (playing four notes)
Trumpet in C (one note)
Trumpet in G (one note)
Three Dulcimers
Triangle
Cymbals
Drum
String quartet (or String orchestra)
Piano

The toy instruments were first played by an assortment of luminaries, including Gerard Hoffnung, at a gala fund-raising dinner. Part of the fun doubtless lay in watching them struggle with unfamiliar instruments and some tricky cues, but the music itself is both ingenious and attractive. In Arnold's Toy Symphony, as in Leopold Mozart's famous previous example, smiles and music happily combine: and this principle, and this work, are both due for a revival.

The Concerto for William Primrose that Arnold had told Roy Plomley about but which in the event never happened was paralleled by a project that failed on the film front. It came from the American producer Sam Wanamaker, who had made his home in London. Wanamaker wanted to make a film about the life of the clown Grimaldi. Knowing of the successful Hoffnung concerts, Wanamaker asked Arnold to consider writing the score. Arnold, though, turned him down on artistic grounds. Anticipating Heinrich Böll's great novel on the theme a decade later, Arnold argued that clowns were not a comic subject, and that the result would be a betrayal. Maybe, too, the subject went too near the bone: as the epigraph to this biography suggests, there was much in Arnold himself of the Clown and Jester, an aspect of himself that he might be willing subconsciously to acknowledge in his abstract music even while declining to do so via this more blatant autobiographical parallel.

Other projects, though, held more appeal. A cross-section through the catalogue assembled by Alan Poulton or Hugo Cole's analytical study of the music reveals at this time a truly incredible versatility. He seemed in the Fifties, his period of maximum productivity, to be able to turn his hand to any occasion that arose. Symphonies and concertos sit alongside vigorous concert openers such as the *Tam O'Shanter* Overture or other introductory flourishes: he could always be relied on for a fanfare. Sinfoniettas, Suites and Dances, even a military march, sit alongside a wealth of chamber and instrumental music and a growing interest in the medium of the brass band, an entirely separate world of music making with its different instrumentation and emphasis on competitions and festivals.

Typical of Arnold's versatility, and of his willingness to undertake occasional music for a specific purpose, was a commission from BBC Television in 1958 for a short piece with an educational function. To show off the components and capabilities of the percussion section, Arnold wrote a five-minute score for three percussionists and piano. The distinguished percussionist James Blades later made it a popular item in his lecture-recitals, arranging it for one player with piano backing, and baptising it in this form at a concert in Grendon Hall, Northamptonshire, in 1961.

Arnold was sometimes asked whether he drew any distinction between the various musical territories in which he operated –

symphonic, film, brass bands, light music – and always denied it. The ebullient Scottish Dances of 1957 which brilliantly take up the mood caught two years previously by the *Tam O'Shanter* Overture and even incorporate a tune by Robert Burns himself that Arnold had earlier also used in a film, *The Beautiful County of Ayr*, were actually a commission from the Light Music department of the BBC, but he did not like the term. He maintained that just because his slow movements, for instance, 'do not indulge in breast-beating,' this does not mean they are not serious or deeply felt. For Arnold there was always a crucial difference between light music and the light touch. Yet he was not ashamed on occasion to own up to a liking for genuine light music. Interviewed by Margaret Howard on his seventy-first birthday he threatened to give an impromptu rendering of Ketelbey's *In a Monastery Garden*.

Not a particularly religious person by nature, he responded to a couple of Christmas commissions. For the BBC at the behest of an acquaintance from his Constant Lambert days, Laurence Gilliam, he wrote in 1957 the Commonwealth Christmas Overture for broadcast around the world. The score calls not just for full symphony orchestra but also for four jazz percussionists and two electric guitars, a bold stroke for the time. Their moment of glory comes when, 'free at last,' they break into an improvisation with distinctly Caribbean echoes and jazzy modulations. Two years later in 1959, to an elegant libretto by Christopher Hassall, he wrote a delightful nativity masque called *Song of Simeon* that remains among the least familiar of his mature pieces. The score has more than an echo in places, particularly in the often syncopated choral writing, of a famous contemporary composer with whom otherwise he felt little kinship, Vaughan Williams. But there are other echoes too: of Holst and Walton in Simeon's first aria, and even of Gilbert and Sullivan in the delicious number for the shepherds (four basses) abiding in the fields.

Nineteen fifty-nine offered further signs of increasing public recognition, particularly in the shape of his appearance on Roy Plomley's popular *Desert Island Discs* programme on the BBC. The composer claimed that he never played the gramophone, even that he was 'anti records' – a sentiment shared by a great many musicians for whom recording is nevertheless an essential part of their livelihood. Arnold's choice of music for that famous if lonely island was nevertheless revealing. It included the end of Stravinsky's Symphony of Psalms, a choice prompted in particular by his memories of performing the piece under the Swiss conductor Ernest Ansermet; Mugsy Spanier playing *Dipper Mouth Blues*, Elgar's *Introduction and Allegro*, and some music by Gustav Holst. There was a nice family connection with Holst, which Arnold was quick to point out: his daughter Katherine was at the time a pupil at St Paul's Girls' School, where Holst had once been Director of Music. From the last two choices, one might fairly deduce that Malcolm Arnold was well aware of his own roots in a distinct English musical tradition.

Nor did he claim at this time to be a particularly political animal – his radical instincts seem only to have begun to emerge with his move in the mid-Sixties to one of the traditional homes of liberalism, Cornwall. There was one aspect of British society, however, which disturbed him greatly, and it duly found an echo in his music. It had indeed already done so, in the eclectic orchestration of the Commonwealth Christmas Overture, but his new symphony went further. In a fiftieth birthday article for the *Listener* in 1971, Arnold described the scenario that was at work.

> The year of my Fourth Symphony, 1960, was also the year of the Notting Hill race riots, and I was appalled that such a thing could happen in this country. The fact that racial ideas have become increasingly strong in this country dismays me even more. In my Fourth Symphony I have used very obvious West Indian and African percussion instruments and rhythms, in the hope, first, that it sounds well, and second, that it might help to spread the idea of racial integration. This of course is only a small part of the work, and is only useful for me to know as a composer.

This ingenuous disclaimer in the final sentence was inevitably ignored by the critics, who disliked what they heard almost to a man. In the arts world generally at this period argument raged over such notions as triviality, vulgarity and lack of taste, and in the person of Malcolm Arnold, music was perhaps feeling the draught at the fringes created a few years earlier by the new theatrical wave for which John Osborne's *Look Back in Anger* acted as the catalyst. The controversy produced a reaction in the composer. Typically, his symphonies had always been separated by substantial gaps, and this was the later pattern too. But only a year after the Fourth Symphony, his Fifth was unveiled in July 1961 by the Hallé Orchestra, with Arnold himself conducting. He commented at the time that 'After the first performance of my Fourth Symphony there were so many things I felt needed to be said musically that I am more than grateful for the opportunity given me by the Cheltenham Festival Society to attempt to say these things.'

Malcolm Arnold's Fifth Symphony is one of his masterpieces, evidently destined to live on long after its creator. For all its sometimes brash surface, it is a work of great depth and considerable subtlety in construction. There are a number of strands in it which can be isolated. Another famous Fifth Symphony, by Arnold's admired Shostakovich, had been conceived as 'a Soviet artist's reply to just criticism'. In his own case Arnold certainly did not admit to any justice, while the reply was combative not in the sense of a submission to authority, but in the sense that he showed an ability to hitch his preferred musical style to prevailing trends. He makes discreet use of Schoenberg's twelve-note methods, even in the angular opening theme with which the Fifth Symphony opens. At the same time the slow movement is dominated by a passionate, Mahler-like melody, eight bars long, that seems to inhabit the world of Hollywood. In his programme note Arnold commented ironically that 'the composer seems unable to distinguish between sentiment and sentimentality', and the slow movement milks this tune for all it is worth. At the very end of the symphony, though, he restates it one final time, only to dismiss it from sight with a bitter unresolved ending on bells and timpani. He was more than aware of the ironic potential behind his fondness for using gestures from popular music.

Then there is the Fifth Symphony's element of commemoration. In his own mind, he was paying a tribute to musical friends who had died young, four in particular. There was Gerard Hoffnung, whose loss was still immensely painful. There was the horn-player Dennis Brain, whose death in a car crash just seemed a tragic waste. The artistry of Jack Thurston on the clarinet had been the powerful stimulus behind not just the Clarinet Concerto and Sonatina but his love of writing for wind instruments in general. And there was David Platenghi, a dancer and choreographer whom he had come to know and love at the time of his Coronation ballet *Homage to the Queen*, and whose irreverent sense of humour had much in common with his own. Memories of all four friends abound, and not just in the elegiac instrumental solos in the first movement; there is anger at their deaths in the scherzo and in the noisy cocktail of the finale as well. This features a typical pipe and tabor tune that is actually a straight lift from his own *Duke of Cambridge March*, written for the centenary of the Royal Military School of Music at Kneller Hall four years earlier. As with the marches in the First and Third Symphonies, though, the intent is again ironic. This last movement therefore has many more layers than appear at first, and forms a worthy finale to a symphony of great musical and emotional complexity. Words alone cannot do it justice.

Words for Malcolm Arnold were indeed a stumbling-block. For a man whose education had included no formal schooling other than two years at the Royal College, Arnold was formidably well-read. Literate and sensitive, in conversation he would often challenge friends on the source of a quotation, or take delight in verbal twists and puns. Perhaps for this very reason vocal settings occupy only a small space in his catalogue and solo vocal settings an even smaller one. He never wrote a full-length opera, the nearest approach being his work with his friend and librettist Joe Mendoza on a possible entry for the 1951 Festival of Britain opera competition. Their chosen subject was the first black ruler of the island of Haiti. But *Henri Christophe*, as it was to have been called, remained on the drawing-board, as much a product of youthful ambition as of genuine dramatic impulse. The surviving sketches suggest that the inexperience of the two men would anyway have made it a daunting proposition to bring off.

Rejection of the synopsis of *Henri Christophe* did not deter Arnold altogether. During the Fifties he completed a one-act opera for the stage and a pair of short works for the fast-developing medium of television. Joe Mendoza again provided him with the libretto for the stage work, a neat adaptation of *The Dancing Master*, a Restoration comedy by William Wycherley. The sheer number of words in the text gave Arnold little room for musical manoeuvre and though there are some neat cameo roles, the opera plumbed no great depths and has never had a professional performance. Its first staging came ten years after Arnold completed the work and even then, in 1962, the orchestral parts were replaced by a piano.

In 1956 Malcolm Arnold enjoyed rather more success with a half-hour piece mounted by BBC Television. Up to that point opera had not rated high in television's concerns, despite a feeling that the medium held considerable potential for a rethinking of operatic conventions. Lionel Salter, then Head of Television Music and in charge of the search for suitable scores, decided that the work Malcolm Arnold submitted, called *The Open Window* and based on a short story by Saki, was sufficiently attractive to please most tastes, even those of a conservative BBC hierarchy. He accepted it for production, booked George Foa to direct and conducted the broadcast himself.

> As it was something he had already written (not commissioned by the BBC) it wasn't specially geared to TV nor, apart from a couple of outdoor shots, did George Foa attempt to open it out scenically; but its chamber character and musical simplicity suited the circumstances of the time admirably. Apart from showing his jolly rubicund face on one occasion, as far as I can remember Malcolm left the production very much to itself . . . The little opera went out live, as did everything at the time, and to my knowledge no recording was made of it.[16]

The Open Window opened another important door in Arnold's composing career, that of television itself. He went on to write the music for a number of series – *War in the Air*, and the signature tunes for *Music for You* and *Gala Performance* for the BBC, and

Espionage and the theme tune of an adaptation of *Hard Times* for ITV – but this was his period of maximum involvement in films, and the senior medium tended to take priority. As for opera, Malcolm Arnold never quite gave up the ambition to write a substantial operatic work. He acquired, and did not surrender, operatic rights to Graham Greene's novel *The Heart of the Matter*, though its tropical African setting and intricate psychological criss-crossing were not an immediately obvious operative vehicle. With an imaginative libretto, though, Arnold could certainly have produced something serious and powerful. For there is no doubt that, even if opera as such eluded him, he remained drawn to the stage and to the dramatic. Instead, the instinct was sublimated by his work in two other fields: ballet, and as was by now obvious, the cinema.

Dame Ninette de Valois, who knew what she was talking about, once described Arnold to his face as 'the finest ballet composer since Tchaikovsky.'[17] He took great pride in the accolade. There have over the years been a great many ballet scores commissioned from and written by English composers, but most of them have lasted only as long as the ballets themselves. Even those that have achieved a life independent of the theatre have sometimes done so because of their composers' achievements in other fields – such as Vaughan Williams, Walton, Bliss or Britten. Malcolm Arnold's first ballet score was very much tied to a specific occasion, and his music for *Homage to the Queen* has been little heard since the Coronation of 1953. Yet precisely because of the significance of the occasion, and because so much was at stake, Arnold laboured mightily to give of his best.

He might almost never have been involved. He had never written a score for ballet before. When the Royal Ballet determined, very late in the day, on a Coronation gala and on choreography specifically designed for the occasion, the first choice for the music was the composer Humphrey Searle, who had already worked with the Company. Searle eventually decided he could not produce a score adequate to the occasion in the relatively short time available. Asked to suggest an alternative he thought at once of Arnold, word of whose ability to work at speed on films had already spread down the musical grapevine, and recommended him to a sceptical Covent Garden. Arnold was summoned to the presence of Ninette de Valois and given his instructions. Not a little alarmed by her formidable entourage he was too inhibited to ask detailed questions. Later, though, he prevailed on Frederick Ashton to write down the precise requirements. This the choreographer duly did, on a sheet of Covent Garden notepaper, in very specific detail, such as: 'Variation – Somes, 3/4 minute, allegretto pesante, 3/4 or 6/8 time' or, later: 'Coda, 3/4 minute, presto, 2/4 time.'[18] Jocular hints on the orchestration were also provided: 'Pas de Deux, grande Adage (mit harps doing overtime)!' But there was a friendly footnote, too, which put composer and choreographer on the same side: 'All this is merely an indication for you and can be departed from at will, and anything altered to suit your musical conception.' The two men got on well and Ashton told Arnold there was one reason he particularly enjoyed working with him at Covent Garden: 'You're the only man in this place who makes me feel thin!' Given the prevalence of French terminology in ballet they took to conversing occasionally in pidgin French, with Arnold complaining that Ashton was incomprehensible because he had a vulgar Marseilles accent.

Discussion of a possible scenario quickly settled on four tableaux portraying four Queens of England: Elizabeth the First, Anne, Victoria, and the new Queen, Elizabeth the Second. Arnold began work immediately, keeping in mind the period flavours Ashton had noted – the first Entrée to be Elizabethan, the second 'Anneish', and so on. He had just ten weeks to complete the music. Problems began to arise when the designer, the young Oliver Messel, claimed that this scenario did not allow him adequately to distinguish the characters in terms of the overall stage design. Variations on the theme of royalty were too much of a restriction. Unwilling to risk further disruption, Ashton gave way, and the scenario was altered, to embrace instead a new theme: The Four Elements. Arnold agreed that the music he had already composed could be made to fit this new theme satisfactorily, and he went on to finish a forty-five-minute score. It is one of his warmest and richest, turning effortlessly on the point of a toe from tenderness to romance to heroic to ceremonial, one moment with the strings swooping in unison, the next with a fragile harp or woodwind solo, the next with the full orchestral resources thundering out the grand finale. Within Ashton's tight framework Arnold enjoyed considerable freedom, and he came up with some delectable moments: for instance, a *pas de trois* in the Water section that suggested Tchaikovsky in its airy lightness, with woodwinds high over featherweight staccato strings, a Water waltz that is pure Arnold, and a noisy orchestral showpiece in the Air section that with its whooping horns and off-beat accents anticipated the world of Arnold's *Tam O'Shanter* Overture. *Homage to the Queen* neatly welded its sequence of sometimes delicate, sometimes exuberant miniatures into a sturdily coherent whole, and fulfilled its ceremonial duties with good humour and superb technical aplomb. *Homage to the Queen* does indeed end with an apotheosis, with Margot Fonteyn as Queen of the Air and Michael Somes as her partner swept off their feet by the entire company in something not far short of a Coronation.

Apart from Fonteyn and Somes the others involved were Nadia Nerina as the Queen of the Earth, with Alexis Rassine as her consort; Violetta Elvin as the Queen of Water, partnered by John Hart; and Beryl Grey as the Queen of Fire, with John Field as her consort. (Among the other dancers was Svetlana Beriosova, for whom, after *Homage to the Queen*, Arnold wrote the score for another Ashton ballet, *Rinaldo and Armida*, which much to his delight he was allowed to conduct himself.) In addition to the Four Elements – through which the *corps de ballet* remained constant – there was an imposing Prelude, to get the whole company on stage at the outset. Arnold took advantage of his position as composer and his privileged access to rehearsal. He made a point of talking to the dancers and of learning what was required of a ballet composer – and conductor. Robert Irving was to conduct *Homage to the Queen*, but Arnold was sensibly looking to the future.

Despite the element of showcase in the occasion and the

Northampton – the 1920s and 1930s

1 Waiting for the Muse

2 With his father, William Arnold, and elder brother Philip

3 With his mother, Anne Arnold (née Hawes)

4 A Secret Garden – with teenage gardener

Wartime

5 The Arnold siblings: Malcolm, Ruth, Aubrey, Clifford, Philip

6 On holiday at Hope Cove, Cornwall, during the phoney war

7 Youthful respect: portrait of Sir George Dyson, Principal of the Royal College of Music 1938–1952, by Anthony Devas

Richmond – the 1950s

8 'Like a tic-tac man on a racecourse' (*The Times*)

9 Rehearsing his First Symphony

10 Official recognition (note the cigarette)

11 Straight into full score, in ink

Sound Barriers – the 1950s again

12 The composer and David Lean watch Muir Matheson conduct the soundtrack for *The Sound Barrier*

13 A small instrument for a big space – with Larry Adler before the Royal Albert Hall première of the Harmonica Concerto

Friends pictured within

14 'That chord is impossible!' – with Julian Bream

15 'A concerto for *two* violins?' – with Yehudi Menuhin

16 'Have you heard the one about the viola player who . . . ?' – with William Walton

17 'A Grand Grand *Grand* Overture, you say?' – with Gerard Hoffnung

Cornwall – the 1960s and 1970s

18 A 'furrener' reflects on his Cornish identity

19 At Padstow, no Padstow Lifeboat in sight

20 The Taxman Cometh – an Arnold manuscript

Norfolk – the 1980s

21 Through thick and thin – with Sir Charles Groves and Dennis Simons, leader of the BBC Philharmonic, at the première of the Ninth Symphony

22 Indian Summer – with the recorder-player Michala Petri

Norfolk – the 1990s

23 As seen by the artist John Minnion

24 A late study by Gina Gutteridge

25 By Oulton Broad

inevitable element of divertissement in the scenario of *Homage to the Queen*, its reception was enthusiastic. The dancing was generally reckoned to be of the highest standard, and Arnold's music was widely perceived as allowing the Company to flower as the occasion demanded. Almost the only dissenting voice was that of the *Sunday Times* ballet critic Richard Buckle, who wrote that the Royal Ballet would have been better advised to have used Glazunov's *The Seasons* for the occasion. Forty years later, the remark still rankled.

The actual proceedings on Coronation Night had a touch of the bizarre. The gala started with the second act of *Swan Lake*, with Margot Fonteyn partnered by Robert Helpmann, who returned specially for the occasion as a guest artist. At nine o'clock there was a pause, during which the new Queen's address to the nation was broadcast throughout the Opera House. Only then was *Homage to the Queen* performed.

Homage to the Queen found a particular fan in another English composer of a slightly earlier generation, whom Arnold barely knew. This was Lennox Berkeley. Years afterwards, Arnold was astonished and not a little flattered to learn that Berkeley had been to see the ballet no fewer than ten times – his admiration was for Arnold's score rather than Ashton's choreography. Eventually, he even asked to borrow the music.

By way of acknowledgement for his work on *Homage to the Queen*, Arnold was invited by Frederick Ashton to compose another work for Covent Garden, which Ashton would choreograph. This was to be a one-act ballet first performed in January 1965, and based on a famous episode in Tasso's allegorical poem *Ierusalemme Liberata*. *Rinaldo and Armida* tells of the enchantress Armida, who lures lovers into her garden to destroy them, but falls in love with one of her victims, Rinaldo, and causes her own destruction. This time, Ashton and Arnold had Svetlanova Beriosova for the title role, and Michael Somes as Rinaldo. Ashton's direction explored to the full the mixture of passion and reserve characteristic of both dancers, who were virtually the only protagonists. In this he was helped by an Arnold score that was often less extrovert and flamboyant than some of its successors –

but which, perhaps for that reason, left less of an imprint. The reviews were not enthusiastic: Ashton's choreography was described as 'fatally chic', while Clive Barnes in the *Observer* was also critical, not of the choreography, but of Malcolm Arnold's score.

Even so, Ashton had sufficient confidence in his composer-collaborator to remember him during a much later project, and to ask for his help. Had Arnold accepted, his career might have taken a very different course. Ashton determined, in 1963, to stage his own version of a popular nineteenth-century favourite, *La fille mal gardée*. He wanted to return to the original musical sources, but needed someone to undertake the necessary research and to work them up into the coherent sequence which he had devised. It meant working over the original scores by Hérold and an anonymous hand, orchestrating and arranging where appropriate. Arnold, under pressure of time from films and evidently not relishing a task that sounded akin to hack-work, declined. John Lanchbery, the resident conductor for the Royal Ballet, eventually took on the task: with what success, all the world knows. Malcolm Arnold, though, was never one to regret lost opportunities, and never begrudged Lanchbery his success. On the contrary,[19] he admired the result enormously.

The first performance of *Rinaldo and Armida* took place in January 1955. A year later, this time to a commission from the Sadler's Wells Theatre Ballet, Arnold enjoyed a happy collaboration with a new choreographer over a work which enjoyed a success equal to that of *Homage to the Queen*, and which, because its subject-matter was not tied to time or place, has easily outlasted the earlier work, *Solitaire*. The ballet helped make Kenneth MacMillan's name and established him as a choreographer skilled at combining fantasy and reality. For *Solitaire* Kenneth MacMillan staged not so much a story as a theme: that of the lonely child unable to make lasting friendships, but happy when memories surface of friendships that succeeded. The staging and choreography were as light, clear and original as the scenario itself, while the music matched the changing moods on stage with almost uncanny precision.

It was not, as it happens, an original ballet score. MacMillan had recognised the dance potential of Malcolm Arnold's two sets of English Dances, and worked out a scenario which required shuffling their original order – and also left him with an awkward gap in the middle. He knew, though, exactly what he wanted and asked Arnold to compose two new dances, a sarabande and a polka, to go into *Solitaire* at the requisite point, using the identical orchestration to the earlier Dances. Arnold was delighted to oblige and wrote the score in under a fortnight. He turned in two miniature masterpieces, fully the equal of their predecessors, the one wistful and grave, the other earthy and vigorous. Rather to their surprise, the Company found themselves with a hit on their hands, and a durable one, with the role of the Girl inherited by a succession of fine ballerinas – Margaret Hill was followed by Elizabeth Anderton, and later by Lynn Seymour. It was even successfully exported on a number of occasions, and the new Sarabande and Polka began to enjoy an independent concert life of their own.

In 1959, Malcolm Arnold became involved once more with the Royal Ballet. In December the company mounted a Christmas show, a kind of Victorian burlesque in the shape of *Sweeney Todd, the Demon Barber of Fleet Street*, with John Cranko as choreographer. The danced sections amounted only to about one third of the whole, which was a wordless mixture of melodrama and slapstick. The danced sections, for a *corps de ballet* of comic policemen, in fact had scant relevance to the gory events of the story, which included Sweeney Todd's hapless victims serving as convenient ingredients for the pie-shop next door. John Cranko was thoroughly at home with the elements of music-hall and revue; others, though, found the entertainment somewhat less appropriate to the dignity of the Royal Ballet.

One other reason for the relatively lukewarm reception accorded to *Sweeney Todd* was that John Cranko was nearing the end of his time with the Royal Ballet and was passing through a period of critical disfavour. Though he remained on the staff for almost another year, *Sweeney Todd* proved to be his last new ballet for the Company before his departure to a post in Stuttgart – where one of his first actions was to invite Kenneth MacMillan to mount his version of *Solitaire* for German audiences, using Arnold's music.

Soon after *Homage to the Queen*, Arnold also worked with yet another celebrated choreographer, the flamboyant Robert Helpmann, on a project where ballet, though important, was only incidental. This was a production of Shakespeare's *The Tempest* that opened at the Old Vic in London on 13 April 1954, with a starry cast that included Richard Burton as Caliban, Michael Hordern as Prospero, Fay Compton as Juno and the youthful Claire Bloom as Miranda. It was a visually elaborate production, with the element of magic played to the hilt, and Helpmann used every opportunity for music. Arnold's score resulted in thirty-five separate numbers, including settings of Ariel's songs and plenty of music for Juno's Masque towards the end. He was allowed a theatre ensemble of nine players and used them in every conceivable combination. Eight years later, Arnold was to spend the latter part of 1962 and the first couple of months of the following year at work on a new commission from the Royal Ballet, which was to reunite him with Helpmann.

Electra was to be Helpmann's first new ballet at Covent Garden since 1946. His cast included several of the current principals in the Company, including Nadia Nerina in the title role, David Blair as Orestes and Monica Mason as Clytemnestra. The action of the drama was ruthlessly compressed into not much more than half an hour, with the result that Electra's murderous revenge on her mother seemed more violent than ever, highlighted as it was not only by a lurid Arnold score but also by stark, gigantic designs in black and white by the Australian artist Arthur Boyd. Surviving photographs show Electra in war-paint, hair streaming, being flung through the air in headlong dives by a *corps de ballet* got up as Spirits of Vengeance.

Arnold's music, though, paid the penalty of being cast in similar mould to a distant predecessor, Richard Strauss's opera on the same subject. He could not have known it at the time, but *Electra* proved to be the last ballet for which he was specifically to write the music. In the late Seventies he worked spasmodically on another score, to a scenario drawn from *The Three Musketeers*, but he never completed it. A decade later still, for Sadler's Wells Royal Ballet, the choreographer David Bintley created a work called

Flowers of the Forest that combined Scottish and classical dancing, also marrying in the process Arnold's Scottish Dances and Benjamin Britten's *Scottish Ballad*. Arnold's score formed the first and more obviously ethnic half, and Bintley was quite content to go for the obvious, such as a drunken dance for the wild modulations and lurching bassoon solo of the second dance. It was in essence, though, a quiet but effective Company ballet, without starring roles for principals and with no strong dramatic scenario, and the Company were happy enough with it to take it on tour to the United States early in 1986. It left Malcolm Arnold feeling that he could, and in his own mind should, have done more. But his attention was too frequently distracted by concert work and by his involvement in a competing medium in which his natural fluency, his love of a good story, and his sheer speed of composition were equally prized: films.

Arnold's entry into the world of the cinema, via the Denham Studio back in the late Forties, was the beginning of a major obsession. He had, after all, been a film fan long before that, all through childhood and adolescence. Working in films became a substitute for opera in particular, and his desk in Richmond-upon-Thames in the Fifties had already seen the birth of an incredible number and variety of film scores, culminating in the Oscar for *The Bridge on the River Kwai*. With only a few exceptions, the music does not exist in isolation from the images against which it was composed; yet by virtue of its sheer quantity Arnold could legitimately claim that this massive expenditure of creative energy was central to his composing identity. Of the twenty or so films on which he worked in the Sixties, none achieved quite the level of public acclamation suggested by *Kwai*'s Oscar and the Ivor Novello award for *The Inn of the Sixth Happiness*.

But there was no let-up in the quality of his inventiveness. Arnold was equally at home continuing to write outrageous burlesque for Frank Launder's St Trinian's comedies, investigating the pipe music of Scotland in preparation for Alec Guinness's heroic exploits in *Tunes of Glory* (1960), studying Indian music for *Nine Hours to Rama* (1962), writing pastiche

German military-band music for *The Heroes of Telemark* (1966), inventing a folk-like Irish marching tune for *The Reckoning* (1969) or, the same year, thinking himself into the musical idiom of his friend William Walton when helping out on *Battle of Britain*.

To take just one score of those written in the Sixties, *Whistle Down the Wind* is characteristic of the freshness and originality that Arnold brought to the medium. This story of three children living on a remote Lancashire farm who think that the stranger they find in a barn is Jesus, when he is really a criminal on the run, required the music to convey first naïvety and innocence, then a certain religious flavour, sentimental perhaps but not cloying, and finally pain and loss of innocence as the children see their idol led away by the police. Arnold did not make the mistake of over-writing the score. Instead, he used a pared-down ensemble of winds and strings backed with guitar and harmonium and a couple of percussion instruments. The distant echo of the Pied Piper motif suggested the inclusion of a human whistler – a function undertaken for the film by its producer, Richard Attenborough. In keeping with his penchant for occasionally using existing material if it provided the appropriate associations, Arnold worked in the Christmas carol 'We three Kings of Orient are', transforming it into a cheerful processional for the scene in which the children take gifts to the man they admire.

Arnold himself[20] called his music for *Whistle Down the Wind* 'one of the best scores I ever wrote' and claimed that the acting of Hayley Mills had been a key factor in his inspiration. (He had the same experience two years later, in 1963, when she starred in *The Chalk Garden*.) John Trevelyan, at this time the Secretary of the British Board of Film Censors, told the composer he thought the title sequence of *Whistle Down the Wind* the finest thing he had ever heard in the cinema, which prompted Arnold to present him with the autograph score. It was no mean compliment, for this was after all the golden age of the British film industry and many other British composers, for several of whom Arnold was happy to express his admiration,[21] such as William Alwyn, Richard Addinsell, Alan Rawsthorne and William Walton, were writing music for it. But Arnold was the equal of them all.

5 : The Padstow Lifeboat

or *Hobson's Choice*

'When Gerard Hoffnung died,
humour went out of music.'

In the mid-Sixties, Malcolm Arnold decided he had had enough of a musical life based on the capital. The pressure of a composing career that embraced serious music, endless films, increasing work for television and radio, together with the need to attend rehearsals of his pieces, and even including some success as a conductor, was proving too much to cope with. The incessant temptations and diversions that were always available threatened to overwhelm the composer. Arnold knew, deep down, that composition was his true *métier* and that his profoundest thoughts were always going to be contained within the classical medium of the symphony – a form in which he felt he still had a great deal to say. Yet 1964 was one of Arnold's thinnest years for composition, until his complete breakdown at the end of the Seventies.

Orchestrally the most substantial piece of this year came with the Third Sinfonietta, op. 81, unambitious in scope as its title implies, but containing at its heart an elegiac slow movement full of bitter-sweet melancholy, succinctly expressed. In a typical gesture of compassionate involvement, he dashed off for Beryl Grey a curtain-raiser, called *A Sunshine Overture*, for a Gala at the Palace Theatre in aid of the Sunshine Homes for Blind Babies.

Otherwise there were only two other concert works, each the result of a slightly unusual commission.

First came a wind-band piece, given the Handelian title of *Water Music* because, like Handel's celebrated Georgian show-piece, it was first performed on a barge. The National Trust, which had become the owner of the Stratford-upon-Avon Canal, had restored the waterway for pleasure-boats and in due course commissioned a piece from Malcolm Arnold for the reopening ceremony. The *Water Music* was played after a performance of *Henry the Fifth* in the adjacent Shakespeare Memorial Theatre on a barge moored at the point where the Canal joins the River Avon. Then later in the year, as a follow-up to the Double Violin Concerto, Yehudi Menuhin asked Arnold for some short pieces to use as encores on a forthcoming American tour. Arnold paid homage to the violinist's interests by basing the second movement, *Aubade*, on an Indian raga, while the finale is a moto perpetuo that pays homage to the outstanding jazz saxophonist Charlie Parker (and thereby anticipates his own Sixth Symphony of 1967, which does the same). Arnold's note in the score carefully explains that the movement 'is based on the type of phrases used by Charlie Parker', suggesting he had tried to capture Parker's characteristic rhythmic inflections.

The only Arnold film in 1964 was *The Thin Red Line*, directed by Andrew Marton to a screenplay based on James Jones's successful war novel of the same name. In 1965 there was no film at all, as composing matters took second place to the ructions in his private life. His first marriage ended in divorce and he quickly remarried. One of Arnold's London friends, acquired via Constant Lambert, was the sculptor-painter-writer Michael Ayrton. Ayrton too was unconventional, original and opinionated, and he adored the music of Berlioz, as did Arnold. He was very close to Isobel Gray, then working as a secretary in the Education Department of the BBC. When the relationship between Ayrton and Isobel Gray ended, Arnold stepped in quickly and she soon became the second Mrs. Arnold.

Isobel Arnold, who was thirty and some twelve years younger than her husband when Arnold married her, was a forceful personality with decided views on how and where she wanted to live. Drawn in particular by Arnold's love of the Celtic fringe, and in what was perhaps a subconscious echo of his escapes to the South-West while studying at the Royal College of Music – and with Isobel already pregnant – the pair went to live in Cornwall, choosing the village of St Merryn, not far from the seaside town of Padstow. They moved into Primrose Cottage, actually a row of three 300-year-old fishermen's cottages converted into a single structure, and for a while Cornwall seemed like an idyll.

Soon after their move, however, came an event that, while its implications were not immediately apparent, was to have profound consequences for the rest of their lives. Their son, named Edward (after Elgar) and Izaak (after Izaak Walton,[1] the author of the fishing classic *The Compleat Angler* – Arnold used occasionally to accompany local boats on fishing trips) was born on 18 July 1965. Slowly it became apparent that his development was not progressing as it should. Eventually they took specialist medical advice.

The discovery that their child was autistic was a shattering blow for Malcolm and Isobel Arnold. The illness was little understood at the time – the term had been unknown to medicine until 1943 – and many confusions and uncertainties still surrounded it. Edward's case was relatively mild compared with extreme examples, where the child's behaviour is severely disturbed or where language acquisition is disturbed, or mental handicap is also apparent. Nevertheless, even mild autism is immensely distressing to parents, precisely because the child's key behaviours cut him or her off from proper parental contact. The social relationships of a child with autism are abnormal. Communication skills – hand and eye contact, response to play – fail to develop. There is a tendency to repetitive activities rather than novelty and imagination. As growth continues, so the child becomes increasingly out of step with the world, unable to think or fend for himself.

Arnold and his new wife had first to cope with the initial uncertainties of the diagnosis itself: autism emerges only slowly and there is often a period of great worry and uncertainty as the child's behaviour fails to develop, deviating not consistently but unpredictably. Unthinkable as it is in the latter years of the twentieth century, autism also had a stigma attached to it, even as late as the Sixties. Poor parenting was assumed to be a major contributory factor and as the biological basis of the illness was not understood, parents could often end up with a burden of irrational blame and self-recrimination. Many marriages were thus put under intolerable strain. Malcolm Arnold's was no exception. For all their love of their son, Malcolm and Isobel Arnold experienced the classic reactions to the diagnosis of Edward's illness: shock, denial, anger, sadness, depression.

Because the illness was slow to emerge, though, these associated emotions were also delayed, for years rather than months. In Edward's infant years the Cornish idyll could to some extent continue. Cornwall has always exerted a spell over artists of all kinds – painters in particular have been lured by its majestic seascapes and skyscapes. Its feeling of being a land apart has also attracted writers, from Robert Stephen Hawker, Charles Kingsley and the eccentric clergyman Sabine Baring-Gould, to the poets Charles Causley and Sir John Betjeman in our own day. *Summoned by Bells* testifies movingly to Betjeman's deep and abiding love for the county and its often mist-bound landscapes and seascapes; he is buried in the little church at Rock, up the coast from Padstow. In Arnold's case there was also the lure of the sea itself – a powerful pull for one who had spent his life until then in the Midlands or in London.

He responded, too, to the Cornish landscape: not just the rugged coastline where sea and cliff meet in often dramatic encounter, but inland. The interior of Cornwall is often unexpected. The shoreline splendour is not repeated. Parts of Cornwall are surprisingly flat and studded with the slag-heaps of the clay-mining industry and the remnants of the tin-mines. The industrial archaeology of Cornwall has its poetic as well as its sociological side. Arnold quickly became sensitive to both. He began to learn something of Cornwall's separate history and to identify with it: 'The Cornish people's sentiment is, underneath, one of hostility to the English because of the "stanners", the tin-miners who suffered at the hand of adventurers, pirates who came and worked people, sometimes children from the age of ten, for two years, paid them little, and then abandoned them when they closed the mines and just disappeared. There's always that resentment.'[2]

And so the rebel found himself comfortably at home, among a people with an oppressed past. Cornwall began to affect his music directly and indirectly. What was to prove one of Malcolm Arnold's most popular and enduring works was the first fruit of this new relationship with a landscape and community. The Four Cornish Dances, op. 91, were finished at St Merryn at the end of May 1966. They were dedicated to his new wife, Isobel Arnold, and rapturously received on their first outing at a Henry Wood Promenade Concert. His programme note for the première expanded on his growing feelings of sympathy, and even struck a political note.

> The Cornish people have a highly developed sense of humour. Many are sea-faring folk, and it is a land of male-voice choirs, brass bands, Methodism, May Days, and Sankey and Moody hymns. The Cornish, despite, or even because of, their great sense of independence, have been ruthlessly exploited. The deserted engine-houses of the tin and copper mines bear silent witness to this, and these ruins radiate a strange and sad beauty.[3]

So the Cornish Dances strike a deeper note than the earlier English or Scottish collections. The four movements are carefully contrasted in tempo and texture to form a coherent whole. The first is a seafaring song of Arnold's own invention which copies the Cornish trick of repetition on a single note. The tune as a whole is a fine and strong one, with a rhythmic hiccough at the end, and each time it comes round it lurches into a new and often hilariously unexpected key, while underneath it runs some highly independent counterpoint in the lower strings. By contrast, the second piece is no dance – it is a landscape in music, ghostly, eerily atmospheric, exquisitely scored. This is the deserted engine-house of the composer's note and over it the bassoon utters a plaintive lament. The Cornish landscape is dotted with such abandoned mines, tragic reminders of Cornwall's past, now objects of bleak beauty in themselves – some with preservation orders on them. 'Sometimes you climb down the cliff and you have a feeling of mystery, of all those people who have suffered, and yet who are still walking out there.'[4]

The third dance raises a different spectre, that of the Cornish Methodist tradition. William Arnold, the composer's father, was a Primitive Methodist, so his son was thoroughly familiar with Cornish religious attitudes and with the kind of hymns sung on Sundays. Again this is not a dance but more of a hymn-tune in the manner of the Victorian hymn-writers Moody and Sankey, warmly scored for brass and requiring a gradual crescendo throughout its length. There is no hint of Arnold parodying Victorian sentimentality, nor any implied condescension towards local custom, but only warm-hearted enjoyment. The final dance is different again, starting with an off-stage procession that distantly recalls, for instance, the 'Fêtes' movement in Debussy's *Trois Nocturnes*. The composer based his inspiration on the Padstow May Day celebrations, using the rhythm but not the notes of the traditional local May dance – 'if I had ever used the tune, I would never have been forgiven!' He was also careful not to confuse the Padstow tradition with another and more celebrated Cornish May Day celebration, the Helston Furry Dance: 'May Day in Padstow is a pre-Christian rite, of strange and mystical origin; nobody knows its exact date . . . I create an impression of the excitement, ending with a huge finale which I always think could be called Bruckner's Day Trip to Cornwall!'[5]

For all their brevity, these so-called Dances – as heard they are more a sequence of miniature tone pictures – are masterpieces of their kind, superbly orchestrated, musically alert to nuances of temperament and landscape, life-enhancing in their openness and honesty. No wonder that arrangements of the Cornish Dances for concert and brass band have proved equally successful; and no wonder that in 1968 Arnold himself added extra brass-band parts to the orchestral version of the third and fourth dances, to take full advantage of local forces available to him for a performance in Cornwall's only Anglican Cathedral, at Truro. The high roof and deep echo added to the Bruckner-like feel.[6]

Once this pattern of involvement within his own community was established, Arnold found that it grew increasingly important to him. The following year, 1967, saw a further example, with a work that was not only local but useful. Specially for the launching of a new lifeboat at Trevose Head (a spot much beloved of John Betjeman), Arnold wrote a march for brass band. *The Padstow Lifeboat*, op. 94, was given its first Cornish performance by local forces, the St Dennis Silver Band with the composer conducting, when Princess Marina came to launch the new boat. A note in the score contains a typical barbed Arnold jest: 'The Padstow Lifeboat has a long and distinguished record. The new lifeboat station is near Trevose lighthouse, whose foghorn varies in pitch between middle C and D. For the sake of musical unity, it remains D throughout this march.'[7]

Sure enough, the note D resounds through the piece to splendid effect, anchoring the piece in the middle of surrounding stormy seas: shivering glissandos portray the fog rolling in over the Atlantic, the main tune marches in high spirits, while a middle section full of furious virtuoso semiquavers requires the principal cornet to fasten his life-jacket, hold tight and pray.

Malcolm Arnold was not a total stranger to brass bands. He had warmed up for *The Padstow Lifeboat* with two Little Suites for young brass players, the first for the National Youth Brass Band of Scotland, the second (even shorter at only seven minutes) for the Cornwall Youth Band, consisting of three character-pieces, Round, Cavatina and Galop. Arnold himself conducted the first performance of no. 2 in Cornwall on Easter Day 1967. Ironically in view of Arnold's later test-piece Fantasy for Brass Band, Peter Gammond[8] describes this Second Suite as 'a genuine attempt to get away from the sometimes over-serious attitudes of brass-band competition music'. And he compares the final movement to a perpetuum mobile by Johann Strauss. The outer movements of both Suites are breezy and extrovert; but the atmospheric cantabile writing of their slow movements is just as successful, if not even richer. It is sad that few of Arnold's contemporaries have been willing to tap this rich seam of British musical life with any regularity, if at all: Benjamin Britten, for instance, wrote nothing for brass band. It takes strong-minded composers such as Arnold, Tippett or Walton to break the mould.

Even to brass players, Thomas Merritt is scarcely a familiar name in British music, not even rating a mention in *The New Grove Dictionary*. So Arnold's *Salute to Thomas Merritt*, op. 98, is at first sight something of a puzzle, until one discovers that Merritt was exactly the kind of personality to arouse Arnold's admiration and respect. Born at Broadlane in the parish of Illogan near Redruth in 1863, Merritt was a typical Cornish oddball. His father, who worked in the tin-mines, died when his son was only eleven, after which the boy was forced to undertake similar work. In spite of a total lack of formal instruction and continuously arduous circumstances, Merritt became a prolific composer, in a solid, sub-Handelian style – hundreds of parochial *Messiah* rehearsals were evidently his main musical education and they lurk audibly in the background of his music. He died on 17 April 1908 at the age of forty-six and a concert to mark the sixtieth anniversary of his death took place in Truro Cathedral, with Malcolm Arnold conducting. Performers outnumbered audience: the Penzance Orchestral Society, Cornwall Symphony Orchestra, St Dennis Silver Band, St Agnes Silver Band and several choirs. Arnold arranged some of Thomas Merritt's music, including a Coronation March for Edward VII written in 1901, and four vocal pieces: a carol, 'Awake with joy, salute the morn', for chorus, two brass bands and orchestra; another carol, 'Send out the Light', for chorus and brass band; and then two anthems, 'The Eyes of All Wait for Thee', for chorus, harp and strings, and 'Awake up my Glory', for chorus and orchestra. Arnold also conducted the augmented version of two of his Cornish Dances, mentioned earlier, and added the specially composed *Salute to Thomas Merritt*.

The *Salute* lasts barely five minutes and consists in essence of an extended fanfare for the two bands and orchestra, who were dispersed around the Cathedral – shades of Arnold's admired Berlioz. In the resonant surroundings of J. L. Pearson's High

Victorian building, the sound was calculated to impress, as much in the quiet passages as in the loudest, for there is an intensity peculiar to the sounds of brass playing pianissimo within a large acoustic. An occasional but not negligible piece, the *Salute* would make an effective curtain-raiser to a performance of either Berlioz's *Requiem* or his *Te Deum*. For local audiences it killed several birds with one musical stone. It resurrected a forgotten local hero. It filled the Cathedral. Arnold lived in Cornwall. It made use of home-grown musical forces. It used a very Cornish ensemble, the silver band. And the occasion was one for amateurs not professionals from outside.

Arnold himself saw this tribute not only as rectifying an injustice. He was being a useful composer again. He was supporting the underdog, and simultaneously fulfilling a role within the community. Such activities were part of a wider concern with humanitarian, even political issues, for the most part unspoken, but which surface in his music particularly around this period. The piece he began to write immediately after the Merritt celebration, the *Peterloo* Overture, is just such a reflection of his wider beliefs.

Arnold's time in St Merryn coincided, after all, with the period that became known as the 'Swinging Sixties', with Harold Wilson in many ways a key figure. (In 1967 the *Daily Telegraph* invited Arnold to compose a setting of a carol, 'This Christmas Night', by Wilson's wife Mary.) As Britain's first socialist Prime Minister since Clement Attlee's government had fallen thirteen years earlier, Wilson's style and attitudes had an influence on many people way beyond the norm. The six years of his first administration, from 1964 to 1970, saw profound changes in the political, social and cultural climate. Arnold was frank about his sympathy with some of them, though he avoided party affiliation:

> A composer depending on orchestras, and on some sort of social formation, has to be something of a political animal. If you have sympathy with the underdog, it cannot be connected with any party. I studied politics deeply, and I've visited Russia and I'm very welcome there, and I'm very welcome in the United States, so I don't want to be pinned down. I should say that what I am is an

> old-fashioned radical, who's studied dialectical materialism and realises the inescapable truth of Marxist and Leninist values.[9]

The *Peterloo* Overture, written in Cornwall in 1968, is in effect a musical declaration of his position, and though it was an occasional piece commissioned by the Trades Union Congress, there is no doubt that Arnold was fully engaged when writing it, for the music has a Charles Ives-like originality and strength of purpose. It is also avowedly programmatic, for Arnold took up the suggestion of Ted Anstey of the Musicians' Union staff and used historical fact as his inspiration. *Peterloo* refers to an incident on St Peter's Fields, Manchester in 1819, when an orderly political meeting attended by some 8000 people was forcibly broken up by soldiers. On the front page of the score Arnold added a note which, as with the Cornish Dances, once again struck a political note in its conclusion.

> This Overture attempts to portray these happenings musically but, after a lament for the killed and injured, it ends in triumph, in the firm belief that all who have suffered and died in the cause of unity among mankind will not have done so in vain.

The music is as unsophisticated as its message: a hymn-like melody stated at the outset is soon interrupted by elements of conflict: at first unpitched sounds of approaching percussion for the procession and later menacing semitones in the brass. The effect of visual discordancy is indeed reminiscent of the Ives of the *Three Places in New England*; and as at the end of another Arnold Overture, *Tam O'Shanter*, there is a glorious apotheosis, the hymn-tune returning in glory with descending scales in the strings, and bells pealing. Nothing clouds or debunks this heroic conclusion, or the warmth of Malcolm Arnold's idealistic, humanitarian vision. 'That piece to the completion of the full score took me about ten days. I don't know how I did it. Alan Rawsthorne used to say I wrote music quicker than it takes to play it. Well it was a compliment coming from him!'[10]

The *Peterloo* Overture is a special case and almost unique in Arnold's music. For the rest, he did not on the whole allow his politics to impinge directly on his music in this way, unlike such committed composers as Shostakovich or, closer to home, Michael Tippett or Alan Bush. Bush, born in 1900 and a lifelong member of the Communist Party, is an interesting case because of his willingness to make a clear distinction between his pure and political music. (Hans Keller maintained that the political implications of Alan Bush's powerful string quartet called *Dialectic* went no further than the title.) The parallel with Shostakovich is more complex and more appropriate, because for most of his composing life apart from a brief period in the pre-Stalinist 1920s Shostakovich was making his protest within an essentially conservative idiom, adapting it to his own ends with the instinct of genius. Arnold, too, was a radical working within a conservative musical framework. Like Shostakovich, he had toyed in his younger days with a more experimental musical vocabulary, only to turn his back on the austerely rigid serial technique practised by Pierre Boulez and his followers in the 1950s, in favour of a musical language still rooted in tonality. This choice of language brought him into potential contact with a much larger public than the increasingly specialised audience of the avant-garde. To this extent, his music is more 'democratic' than that of some of his contemporaries.

Appearances, though, can be deceptive. It was no accident that the composers who stood highest in Arnold's own pantheon were none of them populists, even if one of them, Gustav Mahler, drew heavily on elements of popular Viennese culture. Mahler, together with Berlioz and Sibelius, was something of a maverick figure in his time. All three were outsiders, and stood apart from any continuous line of musical development. As for Sibelius, Arnold declared unequivocally to Murray Schafer that 'the finest piece of music written in the last fifty years is Sibelius's Fourth Symphony, and it never ceases to amaze me from the formal point of view'. Such a statement runs distinctly counter to Arnold's populist streak, represented in the breezy diatonic ebullience of the English and Scottish Dances, for example, as well as his many film scores, and it does not really square with his occasional attacks on the avant-garde. He chose more than once to portray himself as anti-intellectual, a man of the people, but his music often refuted the suggestion – indeed at other times Arnold himself claimed that music is a unique combination of science and art, that there is a necessary intellectual component in composition, and that in his own case it had consisted in a thorough grounding in the rules and techniques of sixteenth-century counterpoint in the style of Palestrina, administered by his youthful first teacher, Philip Pfaff.

From that grounding, Arnold felt confident enough in his own ability to embrace whatever elements he wanted in the prevailing musical culture without compromising his integrity. It may seem odd that, within his output, melodic material of extreme diatonic simplicity should sit alongside material generated by techniques borrowed from Schoenberg, as it does in the Fifth, Sixth and Seventh Symphonies. Arnold, though, was an unashamed eclectic, believing only that the musical end justifies the musical means and that the composer is entitled to use all techniques available to him in the search for the great goal, as he saw it, of musical directness and clarity of utterance. Whatever he may have said on occasion to the newspapers about what he saw as the less acceptable face of modernism – and the two articles reproduced at the back of this biography contain some sharp digs in this direction – Arnold on other occasions revealed his respect, even admiration, for composers on the other side of the musical fence from his own. He told Michael Oliver in 1980 that he envied Webern his clarity of texture and sheer craftsmanship, and that he recognised the abundant lyricism in Alban Berg. He remembered reading and approving, as a student, Ernst Krenek's textbook, *Studies in Counterpoint based on Twelve-Tone Technique*. Clearly Malcolm Arnold's musical credo was a complex one, instinctively felt rather than carefully rationalised. Nor did he believe in talking theory too often, though the first article reproduced on p.166, somewhat inadequately headlined 'I think of music in terms of sound', is a highly articulate summary of his musical thinking throughout his career.

Towards the end of the Sixties, Arnold's work brought him increasing public acknowledgement, first in the South-West, then nationally. In 1969 he was made an Honorary Doctor of Music of Exeter University and in August of the same year he received an honour which by his own account meant even more to him. He became a Bard of the Cornish Gorsedd, taking the name Tromba, Trumpet. He felt immensely proud and flattered by his adopted county when on 31 August 1969 he was duly installed at a ceremony in Liskeard. In 1970 he was appointed a CBE for services to music.

Once Malcolm and Isobel Arnold had settled in Cornwall, the workload soon began to assume its previous gargantuan proportions, because the film studios started to press and the money was always welcome. Nineteen sixty-six, the year of the Cornish Dances, saw no fewer than four feature films, including *The Heroes of Telemark*, *Sky West and Crooked*, the fourth St Trinian's film, and *Africa – Texas Style*. Apart from the brass-band works, 1967 saw no films apart from a short documentary called *North Sea Strike*, but he became involved with television on *The Turtle Drum*, a short children's play with music commissioned by the BBC.

Nineteen sixty-eight, the year of *Peterloo* and the *Anniversary Overture*, a showpiece written for the twenty-first anniversary of the founding of the Hong Kong Philharmonic Society, was likewise quiet on the film scene, but it was an energetic year on another front: the rostrum. He was regularly in charge for all his own premières and increasingly received invitations to conduct other music as well. Since this was an activity apparently at odds with Malcolm Arnold's often-expressed anti-authoritarian political and social attitudes, the ambivalence deserves a brief glance.

Arnold's experience of playing in the LPO and elsewhere under such universally admired figures as Furtwängler, van Beinum, Bruno Walter and a conductor whom he particularly respected, Victor de Sabata, had taught him that the best conductors were not tyrants. The authoritarian Toscanini model was abhorrent to him, since it implied men dominating their fellows, giving them orders, regarding them as servants whose duty is unquestioning obedience. He recoiled from such attitudes, in the army as well as in the orchestra, and he detested them still in conductors –

in particular Malcolm Sargent, of whom he was also suspicious on technical grounds. At the opposite end of the spectrum, orchestras that tried to function under collective leadership have only rarely done so effectively, as Arnold was forced to recognise. The conductor, then, is a necessary evil. He must respect the democratic structure of an orchestra, acknowledge the players' self-respect, above all recognise that they have skills he does not possess. Collaboration rather than command is the ideal. He had found it in other conductors whose work he had experienced directly as a trumpeter: Erich Kleiber, Ernest Ansermet, Clemens Krauss and two English musicians who died before their time, Constant Lambert and Leslie Heward.

Taking up the baton, Arnold was also recognising it as no bad thing for composers to conduct occasionally: to go into the market-place, or bear-pit, and to observe at first hand the reactions of those who must play the notes they have written. Reports of his own performances bear out the success of his particular methods, even though his actual stick technique was described as graphically idiosyncratic and – in a phrase once used by *The Times* – 'like an impatient tic-tac man on a racecourse'. In the 1960s he was particularly active on the rostrum. In 1962 he appeared with the Leicestershire Schools Symphony Orchestra, then just beginning to make an impact as one of the first county youth orchestras under some of the more enlightened education authorities. In 1965 he was unusually busy and his engagements included an appearance at the Proms conducting Tchaikovsky's Second Symphony and the Grieg Piano Concerto.

Opinions were known to differ about Malcolm Arnold on the rostrum. Fritz Spiegl, who played under him as a flautist, felt that he clearly hated rehearsing; and also recalled[11] a live broadcast when the composer neglected to beat the final bar of the slow movement of one of his symphonies, and said after the broadcast that it was probably an improvement! Another flautist, the composer's old friend Richard Adeney, particularly admired his ability to cope with the complexities of film sessions, where the conductor is even more liable to exposure than on the concert platform. In everything he conducted Arnold had decided views on tempo in particular, in his own music above all. He regularly complained that it was played too fast, citing as an example the end of his Second Symphony, which for him could not be slow enough. His recording of the Fourth Symphony on the Lyrita label is notably expansive in all the movements. The BBC tape of his own performance of the Seventh Symphony lasts nearly ten minutes longer than the recording by Vernon Handley with the Royal Philharmonic. Despite the firmness of his convictions, though, and his evident enjoyment of his conducting activities, he only ever listed conducting in his *Who's Who* entry as a recreation. And after 1975 it disappeared even as that, as the pressures of time and health mounted. He continued, however, to list reading and foreign travel as his constant methods of relaxation.

Given his pronounced views on conductors and conducting, it is not surprising to find Arnold describing Sir Thomas Beecham as the greatest he had played under, for precisely those qualities which Arnold himself ranked as any conductor's prime virtues: the ability to make each member of the orchestra feel that his activity is worthwhile, the capacity to inspire confidence throughout the entire ensemble. 'He always got the orchestra sitting on the edge of their seats and playing our best.' He was prepared to recognise that for Beecham 'it was all a big but serious joke'[12] – but the jokes always revolved around words; Beecham never joked with the music. His performances of Berlioz were in part responsible for that composer's profound influence on Arnold. Marvellously as he would have handled it, Beecham never conducted any of Malcolm Arnold's music. Arnold himself never mentioned it. He would have felt, he said, 'impertinent'.

Nineteen sixty-nine involved, in addition to a challenging Proms piece for an unfamiliar combination, three hands at two pianos (Cyril Smith had lost the use of his left hand as the result of sudden depressurisation on an aircraft flight), no fewer than three major film projects, one of which he determined to make his last. *David Copperfield* was a subject close to Arnold's heart, and in his own mind 'the score has some very good stuff in it'.[13] Then, as if in premonition of a later period in Ireland during the Seventies, he wrote the music for a film called *The Reckoning*, directed by

Jack Gold with a screenplay by John McGrath based on Patrick Hall's Irish-based novel *The Harp that Once*. Uncharacteristically he later re-used some of the music and offered an ingenuous explanation: 'I did it for a very special reason. It was going to be, and has been, my last film, and I used it to commemorate that in the Eighth Symphony. To me it's not an Irish tune; but somehow it sounds like it.'[14]

The Eighth Symphony belongs to a later, critical phase in Malcolm Arnold's life. In 1969 in Cornwall there was someone else's film crisis to be dealt with, his old friend William Walton's problems with *Battle of Britain*. According to Arnold's account, he was initially involved in the orchestration, 'and when William Walton was stuck I helped him along'.[15] He was also asked by United Artists to extend the score in places, and the last third of the 'Battle in the Air' sequence is in Arnold's hand. He conducted the orchestra at the recording sessions, only to discover that, despite the intervention of Sir Laurence Olivier, at the last minute Walton's music was largely replaced by a score by Ron Goodwin, 'because the publishers wanted music that would give them a better rake-off . . . Walton was heart-broken by the treatment he received from the film company.'[16]

The two composers had been acquainted for years. Arnold had played in some of Walton's earlier film music when he was in the LPO after the war. Their association had ripened into a firm friendship, with Arnold regularly taking his family to stay at Walton's home on the Mediterranean island of Ischia. On the occasion of a second Walton crisis, when he had to finish transforming his early String Quartet into a Sonata for Strings for Neville Marriner's Academy of St Martin-in-the-Fields in something of a hurry, Arnold offered assistance, knowing this might be the spur Walton needed. The trick worked. He went out to Ischia three weeks later, intending also to work on music of his own, only to discover that Walton had made substantial progress with the Sonata: 'We more or less had a race, meeting for luncheon and dinner and reporting progress. I am sorry to say he beat me by about two days, but after all mine was a quick movement with so many semiquavers.'[17]

Arnold was responsible for arranging Walton's last movement. In March 1972 he was happy to pay tribute to the older composer at the time of his seventieth birthday in a little piece called *Popular Birthday* written for a celebratory concert in the Royal Festival Hall that included a number of similar pieces by other contemporaries; in his piece, Arnold quotes 'Popular Song' from Walton's *Façade*. Also in 1972 he dedicated the Overture *The Fair Field*, op. 110, 'To William Walton with the greatest esteem and affection,' even though the commission had no connection with him – it marked the tenth anniversary of the opening of the Fairfield Hall in Croydon, Surrey. At about the same time Walton completed a set of Five Bagatelles for solo guitar with Julian Bream in mind. The manuscript originally bore no dedication, but Walton later presented it to his friend, writing on it the words 'To Malcolm Arnold with admiration and affection, for his 50th birthday'. The odd phrase in the Bagatelles even sounds like Arnold!

In return, much of Arnold's masterpiece, the Seventh Symphony, was written in Walton's villa on Ischia. They had, after all, much in common. They had shared the trials of writing film music; they loved Italy, Italians and Italian food; each had flirted with jazz, as well as with Schoenberg; and they regarded humour as a distinctly plausible musical ingredient. Walton, too, had appeared at a Hoffnung concert, conducting an extract from *Belshazzar's Feast*. With vast orchestra and soloist assembled on stage, it consisted of a single unaccompanied choral shout: the word 'Slain!'

Friendships such as this one with William Walton were not easy to sustain from deep in Cornwall. Inevitably Arnold lost touch with the influential musical circles of the capital. He was still periodically in the news; most notably when he twice had recourse to the law courts to defend his good name. In 1964 a record company made the bad mistake of confusing Kenneth Alford's original *Colonel Bogey* with Arnold's *River Kwai March*, the sleeve note being open to the interpretation that Arnold's march was not his own. Arnold accepted their apology and asked for a sum of money to be paid over to the Royal Society of Musicians. Two years later the magazine *London Life* implied in a profile of the choreographer Gillian Lynne that Arnold had let her down badly at the last minute over a commission, when the truth was that he had turned down the project as soon as it was offered. Again Arnold took no money other than his costs, accepting that the libel had been inadvertent.

His peace of mind was also occasionally disturbed by financial matters. Tax was on his mind. He even gave vent to some of his frustration on this score in music. In the spring of 1969 the bass Jon Godber, a singer with a taste for the off-beat, had asked the composer for a song that would fit into 'The Invisible Backwards Facing Grocer', his unusual recital programme of 'contemporary British songs to contemporary British texts'. Arnold responded with *The Song of Accounting Periods*, dignified as opus 103, which he finished at St Merryn in January 1969. The text in question, set largely in mock recitative but with bizarre flourishes always on the word 'accounting', is specified as The Finance Act 1965: Part V, Schedule 18, Paragraph 9, Sub-paragraphs (1) and (2). It is, needless to say, a passage of tax jargon incomprehensible to all except lawyers or accountants!

So Malcolm Arnold's period in Cornwall was, in his own words, 'happy but not idyllic – there's nothing idyllic about writing music and bringing up a family'.[18] He continued to love the people and the landscape; but there were the occasional worrying signs. In February 1970 Isobel Arnold was once so worried at her husband's condition that, knowing he had swallowed sleeping tablets the previous evening, she called the doctor in the early hours of the morning. The doctor duly summoned an ambulance and Arnold was taken to the Royal Cornwall Hospital in Truro, some twenty-six miles away. Still in pyjamas and dressing-gown, he walked out in the middle of the afternoon, taking a taxi all the way home again and threatening to register an official complaint. Whether it was a symptom of growing conflicts within the marriage, or just the misunderstanding Arnold later quickly claimed, the episode created unwelcome publicity.

Later the same year, Arnold had recovered sufficiently to collaborate on a major project involving the synthesis of various musical elements which normally hold each other at arm's length. Never one to be put off, and scenting the chance to exploit in practical terms his continued love-affair with jazz, he plunged in wholeheartedly. The end result was the Gemini Suite by Jon Lord, written to a commission from the BBC for a work for pop group and orchestra. Jon Lord was at the time a member of Deep Purple, the group in question; the orchestra was the London Symphony Orchestra, and Arnold, having seen the score, agreed to conduct and did so with enthusiasm. The collaboration went some way further: it extended to the production of a record and video, and Arnold is credited on the sleeve for his 'invaluable assistance', principally on matters of orchestration. The Gemini Suite is a characteristic product of its time, politically correct in its attempt to ignore established artistic demarcations or barriers of brow, and to confront head-on the implicit clash of cultures, musically all brilliant surface.

As the Seventies began Arnold was increasingly overtaken by the desire for a further change. In an article written for *The Listener* towards the end of 1971 Arnold offered some further clear clues to his current state of mind:

> One of the great curses of the present day is our apparent need to be regimented, and I would suggest that we could use the freedom that the arts give for a wide variety of expression in a wide variety of styles, as an antidote to our narrow lives. In this way we shall put a stop to the self-appointed guardians of art presumptuously trying to drag us by the scruff of the neck into the Seventies and Eighties. We are in the Seventies whether we like it or not.[19]

A plea for creative pluralism; a reverse thrust against the pomposity and pretensions of the critics; a bitter lament over the *Zeitgeist*: these birthday reflections were not those of a happy man. He was ready for a more radical break and within a couple of years was actively planning it. But when eventually he moved his family from Cornwall to Ireland, it turned out that he had still not escaped his own worst enemy: himself.

6 : Four Irish Dances

or *Whistle Down the Wind*

'I have never been in fashion, so I can never be out of fashion. This is not a witticism, it is a stoic truth.'

In 1972 Malcolm Arnold left Cornwall and moved to Ireland, settling just outside Dublin at the port of Dun Laoghaire. There were many reasons for the move, among them the need for a fresh start creatively, now that films were effectively a thing of the past. Ireland also appealed to him partly because it did not imply a total break with the roots he had put down in Cornwall. He continued to see himself as a Celt and to recognise his Celtic side in his creative instincts. For him, Ireland still represented a land of saints and scholars. He liked the pre-Christian toughness of Celtic culture; but he knew better than to be taken in by the image of shamrocks and leprechauns. And in Ireland, he reckoned, he stood a chance of feeling comfortable, unthreatened. 'It made me very much aware again of the underdog. The Celtic in Ireland made me aware of the strength of our pre-Christian origins, which are from the sea. Everywhere I have lived, Britain, Cornwall, and Ireland, I hope a little of that country has rubbed off on me, and made me tolerant.'[1]

And there was a further reason to think of going across the Irish Sea. His son Edward was now eight years old, with a future still very unclear as a result of his autism. It is hard to remember, at the end of the twentieth century, how little understood illnesses of the mind were until comparatively recently.

Autism is now assumed to be largely biological in origin. The Dustin Hoffman film, *Rain Man*, brought about an extraordinary shift in the popular perception of autism, dispelling misconceptions and the remnants of stigma. Even so, there is still neither a proven remedy nor proven treatment; a number of therapies of different kinds are practised, with variable degrees of success. They were largely undeveloped when Edward Arnold was a boy. Malcolm and Isobel Arnold were thus facing a future that combined distressing uncertainty and unjustified guilt. It is also clear now, as it was not then, that autistic children are not necessarily of below average intelligence. Other fears felt by their parents included the threat of epilepsy, which occurs in a high percentage of such children; and the suspicion that autism might be genetically borne, making the possibility of having further children unwise, even dangerous. Institutional back-up, in the shape of special schools, counselling, sheltered accommodation, was not developed – particularly in the South-West. Arnold had heard that these things were better ordered in Ireland. He knew that Maria Montessori, the founder of the Montessori methodology, with its regime of patient individual stimulus, had been active in Ireland and that some of the Irish Montessori schools had achieved remarkable results. Autistic children often possess islets of ability untouched by the illness; music, Arnold's own chosen art, is a common one. Maybe the Montessori method would give his son more stimulus than Cornwall could offer. He decided to see for himself.

Arnold spent two months in Dublin, staying in the luxurious Gresham Hotel, looking at schools and houses and at places to live. He liked what he saw and in mid-1973 Isobel and Edward joined him. They lived for nearly three years in a house called Meadowcroft, on The Hill in Markstown, Co. Dublin, moving in 1975 to De Vesci Terrace, Dun Laoghaire. Musically he did not stand still, continuing during altogether seven years in Ireland to concentrate on concert music, exploring the wider emotional range that had already surfaced in his Cornish pieces, such as the

Concerto for Three Hands (for Cyril Smith and Phyllis Sellick), the Viola Concerto, and the orchestral work which is the most effective synthesis of the various voices of his Cornish period, the Concerto for 28 Players, which is also a virtuoso showpiece for chamber orchestra.

Ireland may have been partly intended as an escape from the endless pressure of work, but certainly in his own mind the composer did not see it as running away from another source of anxiety which – as with the song for Jon Godber – had come to haunt him. He resented the suggestion, hinted at in one or two newspaper reports, that his choice of Ireland for the next Arnold home had anything to do with the burden of taxation. The Irish tax system was known to favour creative artists, but Arnold was well aware that to decamp for that reason alone was more likely to be harmful than the reverse. The country also offered him a certain amount of necessary solitude in which to work, for though a gregarious man, as the pattern of his moves suggests, Arnold also needed to be able to exclude the world at will: 'Vaughan Williams said you should be able to compose with a brass band practising next door. But Vaughan Williams was a very wealthy man, and never had to!'[2]

Certainly there were fewer visitors from London and elsewhere, though the consequences were not wholly as foreseen: thrown back on their own resources, in a pattern all too familiar from his first marriage, relations between Malcolm and Isobel Arnold rapidly became strained. It was perhaps no coincidence that the only score which Arnold wrote for stage or screen during his Irish period was the theme music for a Granada Television adaptation of Dickens's novel *Hard Times*. Instead, if the iron had begun to enter the soul of Malcolm Arnold while he was contemplating the tin-mines of Cornwall, his Irish encounter with the Celtic fringe resulted almost straight away in a concert work with no aura of twilight mystery and unseen voices, but full of dissonance and anger, violent outbursts of orchestral fury and extreme contrasts of light and dark: the Seventh Symphony, op. 113, finished in Dublin on 9 September 1973.

This symphony is the diametric opposite of everything that the composer's public image leads one to believe. It is also one of his greatest works and one of the finest symphonies the twentieth century has produced; properly played, it can be overwhelming in performance. It must be heard in the flesh; loudspeakers tame the huge, elemental forces it unleashes into shadows of themselves. It embraces chaos, disorder, unreason, of the kind Vaughan Williams confronted in his Fourth and Sixth Symphonies. It therefore makes not the least attempt to be ingratiating. Nowhere is a melody spun out for its own sake; instead it will always be geared to the symphony's uncompromising logic. Arnold provided the Seventh with a startling preface that may or may not be accurate as far as it goes – which is not very far. More than once in his career he had done the same, partly out of impish humour, partly out of a belief that the workings of the composer's mind on a technical level are irrelevant to the listener: 'A strong intellectual background to even the most trivial piece of music to me is a necessity, but it is very secondary. I have little patience with the music that I listen to out of a sense of duty, which puts forward its technical basis as the reason for its existence.'[3]

With the Seventh Symphony, though, his introductory note is emotionally evasive. He described the symphony as a 'loose musical portrait' of his three children, Katherine, Robert and Edward, to whom the work is dedicated. This portrait may have been his starting-point, but it was not the finishing-post. Nor is Arnold's Seventh Symphony, for all its family links, a *Symphonia Domestica* in the manner of Richard Strauss. The work's proportions are close to those of Mahler, or Shostakovich. When Arnold himself conducted a performance of the Seventh with the BBC Symphony Orchestra, he took over fifty-five minutes, though Edward Downes, Charles Groves and Vernon Handley, each of whom has brought his own differing emphasis to the work, have generally been closer to forty-five minutes. A further Mahler parallel is provided by the presence, in the large battery of percussion, of a cow-bell. In Arnold's mind this instrument came at the time of writing to occupy a symbolic role. He referred to its resolving the tension at the end of the first movement, and to its last appearance representing hope: 'If it is only a cow-bell, at least it is something.[4]

The scale of the Seventh Symphony is so huge that, evidently, the conciseness of the Sixth was not here an artistic aim; instead, conflicts and their resolution require time to unfold. The first two movements are the most complex pieces structurally that Arnold wrote, and the opening movement in particular is different in kind from anything that had preceded it. Previously conflict had arisen out of ordinary musical contrasts; here it is of the very essence and a battle-chart could equally well be drawn up for Arnold's violently-contrasted themes as for his harmonic collisions. Thematic originality keeps pace with the violent harmonic clashes he engineers; Arnold's control of his material is superb, with the climaxes magnificently judged – the most terrifying moments are reserved for the recapitulation. The periods of relaxation – for there is at least one theme that represents something approaching serenity – are carefully placed also. The end of the first movement is despairing, savage.

The second movement is headed andante con moto, but its motion is heavy, even ponderous and throughout its length there is no respite from the previous tensions. The stark solo-trombone theme, one of a pair of themes stated near the outset, is another illustration of Arnold's highly individual use of serial technique. It winds its way through all twelve notes of the scale, and the nod to the Second Viennese School is appropriate for Arnold's grim intensity here, suggesting an echo of the death-haunted finale of Alban Berg's atonal opera *Wozzeck*. Near the end of the movement, after a savage and chaotic accelerando, the music comes momentarily to rest on a grinding dissonance, marked to be played as loudly as possible. The bleak, slow bassoon solo that follows brings no relief though, and this shattering movement ends in the only way it can, with the instruction *morendo* (dying away) – not frequent in Arnold's music – over the last two quiet chords on low strings.

Among the critical brickbats that were cast at Arnold from time to time, and which caused him much depression, was the suggestion, often made at the outset of his career, that he suffered from a 'finale problem'.[5] What sort of resolution does the finale of the Seventh Symphony offer? In its shape it is a palindrome, A – B – C – B – A, with A the most substantial element, which slips first into a six-eight allegretto, B, and then accelerates still further into an allegro, C. There is a high degree of differentiation between the different elements in terms of rhythm, harmony and orchestral colour, with the B section giving the harp a proper solo, tune and accompaniment, suggesting the possibility of easy diatonic melody and uninterrupted movement. Likewise the central allegro starts out as a descendant of the typical fife-and-drum episodes of the earlier symphonies, a symphonic version of a rustic Irish folk dance. In terms of Arnold's own programme, it is included to represent his autistic son Edward. Edward Arnold as a child loved the Irish folk group The Chieftains; yet as the dance develops their carefree spirit is quickly dissipated. The gradual return of the darker music from the opening of the movement progressively clouds the horizon – though the repeat of the opening is not complete. It is cut short by the cow bell, a unifying factor in the symphony, and one which assumes the power to silence discord.

But does it suggest the hope that the composer himself has been seeking? The effect on the listener at the end of the Seventh Symphony is more like one of stalemate. The primitive force of the preceding two movements lingers on long afterwards, making hope difficult and suggesting an emotional and intellectual upheaval of near-pathological intensity. In the complex equation of life and music that makes up the biography of any composer straightforward parallels are hard to draw; but it seems nevertheless clear that in the Seventh Symphony, Malcolm Arnold's difficult path, mental and physical, in the latter half of the 1970s is here anticipated in music of the utmost power and intensity.

The Seventh Symphony set a pattern for Arnold's Irish years. There was less direct involvement in the community than there had been in Cornwall, or than there was to be in Norfolk later, in the Eighties. There was less emphasis on being a 'useful' composer and no extended involvement with amateurs or schoolchildren, with the exception of the 1976 cantata, *The Return of Odysseus*. Nevertheless, in various ways he gave back to the Irish as much as he took and there was no let-up in his admiration for the Celtic spirit and the independent, unsubmissive Celtic mind.

His publishers saw the success of the English, Scottish and Cornish Dances and pressed for their Irish equivalent. Unwilling to repeat himself, Arnold was cautious, and though he contemplated and indeed began a set of Irish Dances in 1978, they did not appear until 1986. (They were eventually to be dedicated to the chairman of Faber Music, Donald Mitchell, a long-standing friend and the author of one of the first serious essays on Arnold's music.) Characteristically, Arnold later felt that he had perpetrated an injustice to the one nation not so far included in the sequence, and in 1989 duly completed a set of Welsh Dances.

Welsh and Irish elements sat side by side in an exquisite miniature finished in Dublin in May 1975, the Fantasy for Harp, op. 117. This was written for the eminent Welsh harpist Osian Ellis. Though the writing is linear and simple throughout, the 'Lament' and the central 'Nocturne' in particular both have a touch of Celtic melancholy about them. The Welsh Arts Council commissioned a work at about this time, too, and the resulting Flute Sonata was finished in Dublin in 1977. For once it was not intended for Richard Adeney, but for James Galway, who played it first in Cardiff, but thought little of it and did not play it again. True to his long friendship with Arnold, Richard Adeney gave the first BBC broadcast. An uncharacteristically serious note in the score sheds light on Arnold's general musical thinking around this time.

> There are so many works for the flute which are solely vehicles for instrumental virtuosity that I have attempted to write a piece where the musical element is more to the fore. Although this is a virtuoso work with a particular virtuoso in mind, as are all my solo pieces, it endeavours to be as interesting musically as I can possibly make it. Over the past several years I have tended to write in free fantasy form, with the exception of my Seventh Symphony and Second String Quartet. I have chosen the sonata form for this piece because there is such a lot of music in free forms for the flute. It is a sonata in the sense of a violin sonata, or a piano sonata.[6]

It cannot be claimed that the resulting work has any strong Irish associations other than the link with James Galway, though the slow movement has a few touches characteristic of Arnold's Dublin period. The first movement is precisely as the composer states, an extended sonata movement complete with first, second and even third subjects and a genuine development section with major and minor keys locked in conflict. The andantino that follows is only four pages long, yet it has an unexpected strangeness. Here as elsewhere – and it happens in Malcolm Arnold's music from all periods – the regular beginning is deceptive: the textures begin to disintegrate and the music eventually becomes almost motionless, with the flute becalmed on the note A, repeated many times over, before fading into nothing. The finale, though, turns its back on any further problems. The model for this virtuoso exercise in ragtime is Scott Joplin, who was then enjoying a new lease of life, thanks primarily to a best- selling record by the pianist (and Bach scholar) Joshua Rifkin. A couple of brief interruptions threaten drastically to change the mood; but they turn out to be a self-mocking joke and the Sonata ends in pyrotechnics of the kind that James Galway has always relished.

Another Irish work offered a transatlantic link. In the Flute Sonata, Arnold was borrowing a formula he had used once before in Ireland, with equal success, again in a solo wind work: the Second Clarinet Concerto finished three years previously in 1974. The overall shape of the clarinet piece is very similar, even down to the foot-stamping finale. It was written for the American clarinettist Benny Goodman, who throughout his long career was happy – like Malcolm Arnold – to have a foot in both camps, popular and classical. Given his soloist's unique talents, Arnold took full advantage. So at the appropriate moment in the first movement the soloist is instructed to 'improvise a cadenza, as jazzy and way out as you please, based on the Concerto's themes'. In his recording, Benny Goodman is in fact sensibly restrained and brief at this point – possibly because one of the themes in question just happens to cover all twelve notes of the chromatic scale already! Even so, Schoenberg's ghost would have turned a whiter shade of pale had he been listening. For a much later performance, at the 1993 Proms, the clarinettist Michael Collins commissioned a cadenza from another composer, jazz enthusiast and Arnold admirer, Richard Rodney Bennett.

Oboe, clarinet and horn are all given counter-melodies of their own against the clarinet protagonist in the slow movement. Once again there is a rootless and virtually athematic passage in the orchestral accompaniment, before the return of the diatonic main theme. And as in the flute work, the finale invites the clarinettist to let his or her soloistic hair down in a cheeky, fancy-dress ragtime parody. Though it mocks the clichés of jazz, it is devoid of malice or mischief and Arnold subtitled it 'The Pre-Goodman Rag'. His dedication to Benny Goodman on the title page spoke of 'admiration and affection'; both are reflected in this finale's display of uninhibited musical high-spirits.

After the concerto for Benny Goodman came a period, in Dublin, of untypical inactivity. It was to be nearly a whole year before his creative juices began to flow freely again, during which time the strains on his marriage began to tell alarmingly. And he began, too, to be increasingly aware of the effects of his self-imposed isolation. In particular, work from the BBC shrank to a trickle, although his conducting of the first British performance of the concerto for Benny Goodman – with Benny himself as the soloist – was recorded and broadcast.

What with his various commissions and Prom engagements over the years, Arnold had become a wry observer of the BBC's characteristic behaviour and when, as periodically happened, the future of the Proms was being vigorously discussed, with the notion that they were ripe for privatisation, Arnold penned a terse note to *The Times*, asking to be put first in the queue of prospective purchasers. What pleased him about the letter's appearance was not only its condemnation of the BBC's short-sightedness, but the fact that the Thunderer had printed a letter from Eire – no mean achievement, he reckoned. Arnold was certainly prepared on occasion to become a signatory to public statements on musical topics, joining younger colleagues such as Peter Maxwell Davies, Paul Patterson and George Benjamin in a letter to the *Independent* about a proposed withdrawal by the

Inner London Education Authority of funding for peripatetic music teaching in the capital. In 1977 he joined Yehudi Menuhin, Colin Davis and John Dankworth among others in writing to *The Times* about the inadequacies of government funding of the arts.

As far as the BBC was concerned he began to feel increasingly hurt by what he felt as his undue neglect. In the Fifties and Sixties he had done fairly well by the broadcasters in terms of commissions received. Half a dozen requests from the Third Programme were fulfilled: the second set of English Dances, the Commonwealth Christmas Overture, the Fourth Symphony, the Concerto for Two Pianos (Three Hands). Arnold was up among the leaders, and he had done well, too, by the emerging medium of television, collaborating on *The Open Window*, *The Turtle Drum*, *Parasol*, and the educational piece for James Blades, *Concert Piece for Percussion*.

There is no doubt, however, that the arrival at the BBC in 1959 of William Glock as Controller, Music, initiated a sea change in the Corporation's attitude to living British composers, a change that was not necessarily going to operate in Malcolm Arnold's favour. In the case of other composers, previously neglected, sudden reversals of fortune were experienced. In their biography of Elisabeth Lutyens, Meirion and Susie Harries claim that the years 1962 to 1971 'were the period of her greatest critical approval and acceptance as part of the British musical scene', where previously she had scarcely been performed at all. And they attribute this change exclusively to Glock and the BBC.

> The 1950s, in Glock's view, had seen the Second Viennese School and composers like Liz [Lutyens] disgracefully neglected, and he proposed to correct this with a policy of 'creative unbalance', giving serial music, especially that of Schoenberg, an 'unnatural prominence' in its turn. His reading panel was more 'advanced', including Humphrey Searle, David Drew and Iain Hamilton, and he dropped what he described as 'Spa repertory' – the dread spectre of 'Cheltenham music' raising its head again, only to have it lopped off. Glock deflected the BBC's gaze from Honegger, Rubbra and Frank Martin, and directed it towards Schoenberg, Webern, Stravinsky and Gerhard.[7]

Until the arrival of Glock at the BBC, Malcolm Arnold had always appeared regularly at the Proms, often doubling as composer and conductor, and the appearance of this natural communicator was invariably greeted with loud cheers from the Promenaders themselves. Post Glock, *propter hoc*, and his appearances diminished. In his *Companion to Twentieth Century Music*, Norman Lebrecht identifies Malcolm Arnold and Andrzej Panufnik as the two principal casualties of the wind of musical change that blew through Portland Place in the Sixties and Seventies. Despite their periods in the wilderness, though, each composer ended his career with a knighthood. Robert Simpson, too, has documented[8] the way in which the BBC's commissioning policy began to favour a narrower spectrum of modernist composers.

Glock's successors at the BBC were Robert Ponsonby and John Drummond, neither of whom regarded Arnold's music with much more enthusiasm than their predecessor. With one exception, his appearances at the Proms became almost tokenistic, the joker in the pack. This was even true for the *succès de scandale* he achieved when Glock offered him a high-profile appearance at the Last Night of the 1970 Proms.

The requirement was for an alternative to Henry Wood's traditional Fantasia on British Sea Songs that would be less jingoistic, more contemporary, and yet retain an element of audience participation. Modernity was achieved by three unison repetitions, each time to the same simple diatonic tune, of the hymn to freedom of the American Civil Rights movement:

> On the road to freedom
> We shall not be moved,
> Just like a tree that's standing
> By the water side.
> We're brothers together,
> We shall not be moved.

In line with an earlier piece such as his *Song of Freedom*, the appeal of these admirable if naïve sentiments to the composer is no surprise. They were, too, well chosen for the youthful enthusiasm of the Promenaders. The orchestral introduction and interludes between the verses are of no great moment, though the last of them, with discordant brass fanfares and heavy percussion, has a distinctly militaristic flavour and doubtless represents the threat and tyranny of war. Grafted on to the *Song of Freedom* are two more traditional elements: first, the sailors' hornpipe, now written in a teasing 5/8 time, a superb joke that threatens to but never quite actually does outstay its welcome. Then, very brutally, we are flung into the last couplet of Rule, Britannia. Never being a slave may be a kind of equivalent to treading the road to freedom, but the jingoism of ruling the waves was not really dispelled. The publicity was endless, the Promenaders loved it – but the Fantasy fell between one too many stools for comfort, and the BBC has been disinclined to revive it.

After the storm over the Fantasy had died down, Arnold was effectively forgotten by the commissioning powers at the BBC, until the sorry mess over the Ninth Symphony in the 1980s. Invitations to conduct began to dwindle as well. He did, though, make one impressive visit to Studio 1 at Maida Vale, to conduct the BBC Symphony Orchestra in the first broadcast of his Seventh Symphony. The tape reveals a performance of tremendous power and individuality, that lasted not far short of an hour. The broadcast was tucked away in a midweek afternoon. It passed almost unnoticed, and he retreated once again to Ireland.

There was an Irish link in Arnold's next work. He chose a short piece by the earlier Irish composer-pianist John Field as a starting-point for his inspiration. To give it its full title, the *Fantasy on a Theme of John Field* for piano and orchestra was written for the pianist John Lill and first performed by him, not in Ireland but in London, in 1977. The Fantasy turns out to be much more than the piece of Irish nostalgia that the elaborate title might imply. Along with the Seventh Symphony and the Second Quartet, it is one of Arnold's Irish-born works in which light and darkness, sweetness and violence mingle in exaggerated contrast. Living in Ireland may have suggested John Field as a source, but there was another reason as well:

> I first knew John Field's music when as a small child I learnt his beautiful Nocturne in B flat. The theme I have used is the Nocturne in C, and I have tried in the composition to get something of the atmosphere of the main cities he lived in: Dublin, London, St Petersburg and Naples. All four cities I know and love well. This is not programme music in any sense, in fact it is a piano concerto in one movement.[9]

This is another piece of Arnold disinformation, true up to a point, but masking the emotional substance of the score. Arnold's notion of the piano concerto is here the Romantic one, the concerto as vehicle for conflict between the soloist and orchestra. The single movement embraces thirteen different sections including a cadenza, and Arnold again used the form that he found gave him the structural flexibility he enjoyed, the free fantasia. The piano stands for light, against the orchestra's destructive forces of satire and irony; in fact the maestoso conclusion is radiantly optimistic, when the orchestra finally and for the only time takes over the piano's Field-based theme, which the soloist has been doggedly asserting from near the beginning.

Until this point, the John Field tune has been ruthlessly assaulted from all sides. The nearest hint of its intrusion into the introduction, a Shostakovich-like march with the side-drum rampant, is dramatically overwhelmed by the orchestra, which remains glued to other themes and other keys. The principal battleground, though, is a chain of linked sections, getting progressively faster, where fragments of the Field Nocturne appear both in brilliant, almost nightmarish writing and in enforced gaiety, such as in a jazz-style parody. Field the Irishman wins in the end, but the Fantasy is no more a tribute to nineteenth-century aesthetics than it is the naïve travelogue of the composer's programme note. The seeds of destruction are there for all to hear.

Those who during Arnold's stay in Ireland had hoped for another rumbustious set of orchestral Dances were doomed to disappointment from the start. The Irish muse tends towards vocal as much as instrumental expression. Nor did Malcolm Arnold regard traditional Irish music as easily imitable; his ear told him that it was not and that its elemental quality was not to be aped, parodied or exploited, but required deep understanding. The Seventh Symphony was a calculated risk. And Arnold once paid a spontaneous and unexpected tribute[10] to a native Irish composer who had grappled with this very problem, Sean O'Riada. O'Riada died in 1971, before he was forty. Arnold maintained that, had O'Riada lived, he might have done with Irish traditional music what Bartók did with traditional Hungarian music.

The closest Arnold himself came to achieving this kind of synthesis was in some pages of another Dublin work, the Second String Quartet of 1975, which along with the Seventh Symphony and the John Field Fantasy contains some of Arnold's strongest and most powerful music. Bartók is one of the influences behind it, as he had been with the First Quartet a quarter of a century earlier: 'I used to think of music in terms of Bartók's quartets – I admire them tremendously. But it struck me that to carry the emotions they express into everyday life – frenzy and despair – would be raving lunacy.'[11]

Bartók and Arnold share an attribute in the writing of quartets, one which would have aroused the suspicions of Hans Keller, who was always at pains to stress the links between quartet-playing and quartet-composing. Neither was a string player and their works in the medium fall into Keller's category of quartets 'whose substance and texture were simply addressed to the psychology and acoustics of the concert hall'.[12] The two Arnold quartets are both public statements of this kind, yet the Second Quartet in particular, like a near example, Britten's Third (and final) Quartet, is a wholly uncompromising and deeply characteristic piece of self-expression.

That 'public statement' took place first in Dublin Castle on 9 June 1976, by the Allegri Quartet. It is dedicated to the then first violin of the quartet, Hugh Maguire – himself an Irishman with an enthusiasm for the folk fiddle, which provided the composer with a pretext for one of his bolder inventions at the beginning of the second movement. The string quartet does not automatically have to be the most personal and intimate of forms, but it has often acquired a confessional character and Arnold is no exception to this rule. The tone of the dialogue in the first movement is serious, like intelligent conversation; soon it turns to furious argument, with angry semiquavers in all four parts and much contrapuntal imitation and dissonance. The echo of Bartók is strong. When the argument eventually subsides, the brief recapitulation ends on an inconclusive note, before the first violin launches into an Irish reel! But this banal tune is soon enough almost physically assaulted by bitonal outbursts from the other instruments and this furiously explosive energy is sustained throughout the second movement. This is angry music, similar in tone to that of Arnold's admired Shostakovich in his Eighth Quartet, already a repertory piece by this time.

After this, the andante is bleak and bare in its lonely two-part beginning; there is an easing of tension, however, in the middle of the movement, with a very simple tune, harmonised with much warmth and marked to be played quietly on the fingerboard. In spite of its presence and later repetition, it is with the sinewy counterpoint of the opening that the movement ends, 'tough, desolate and profoundly communicative'.[13] It is up to the finale to resolve the complexities and ambiguities of this intricate, personal music.

In fact the finale offers a pair of solutions: a long-breathed theme over a murmuring accompaniment whose later contrapuntal treatment seems to hark back to the less disturbed world of another Arnold string work, the Double Violin Concerto for Yehudi Menuhin written some thirteen years earlier. Then the alternative emerges, more aggressive and short-breathed, dominated by eerie harmonics and a jagged four-note fanfare. The music accelerates precipitately before collapsing on to a final slow section consisting of a simple song-like theme in the first violin. It is hardly a Hollywood sunset, more a temporary suspension of hostilities as evening falls. Neither side can therefore claim victory. Arnold's Second Quartet is a disturbing work to hear; beautifully crafted for the combination, it is on a par with the best of contemporary quartets – those of Britten, Simpson and Shostakovich – and offers an insight into its composer's mind at full stretch.

*

Some at least of the turmoil in these turbulent Irish scores is due to Arnold's personal circumstances. The pattern of his first marriage repeated itself. Attacked by increasing bouts of depression and saddened by the death of his ninety-year-old father William Arnold, he took refuge once more in alcohol, and his second marriage disintegrated. Eventually he attempted suicide: 'I took every pill in the house and washed them down with a bottle of Metaxa brandy – which is very very good, isn't it? Magnificent. When I came round, in the Dublin Hospital built by Dean Swift, I was surrounded by the faces of Irish nurses. I am dead, I thought. This is Heaven; but where the hell am I?'[14]

He was nursed back to some semblance of health and sanity by a loving Irish friend, Deirdre Ryan. But when, eventually, he went home, it was obvious his marriage was over.

In Ireland, before the marriage collapsed, he wrote a rare solo vocal setting of two Donne poems and though the first, 'The Good Morrow', is a reflection on the ecstasy of discovery-through-love, the second, 'Woman's Constancy', is a darker meditation on falsehood. Its climax, 'Vain lunatic, against these 'scapes I could dispute', is set with bitter accuracy, and Arnold also creates a musical sting in the tail to match Donne's suggestion that one tactic against female inconstancy is for the male to behave likewise. Even the cantata that he wrote in 1976 for the Schools' Music Association, *The Return of Odysseus*, turns out to have an ironic twist in Patrick Dickinson's libretto. It tells of the reunion of Ulysses and Penelope – but not before she has heard rumours of the hero's possible seduction by Calypso.

> Odysseus spent his daytime weeping,
> Out by the empty sea,
> He wept for his wife, till the sun was setting,
> And Calypso called 'It's time to be getting
> In bed with immortal me'.

And there was one major project Arnold worked on at about this time destined as a result of his collapse to remain unfulfilled, a full-length ballet based on Alexandre Dumas's *The Three*

Musketeers. Only unorchestrated sketches and fragments exist. By the time Arnold was well again, the deadline was past, the commission had lapsed, and he himself was disinclined to renew contact with a project with unhappy memories.

Yet the pathetic fallacy, though tempting, is dangerous: like most composers, Arnold was entirely able to produce scores untroubled by personal circumstances. The works written in Ireland for Richard Adeney, James Galway and Osian Ellis are all adequate testimony, as also is the clarinet concerto written for a great American musician, Benny Goodman.

Something in Arnold responded to the free and uninhibited temper of the United States and he always regretted not knowing the country better. Accepting an Honorary Doctorate at Miami University in Ohio, he told his audience that he wished he had been a more frequent visitor. There had been strong links: the music of Louis Armstrong, the love of jazz, the homage to Charlie Parker in the Sixth Symphony, the occasional sly nod at ragtime, working in and for films and film men, receiving an Oscar. There was a time when, metaphorically speaking, he was living in Hollywood when he was actually at his old desk in a London suburb. There are echoes in Arnold of Charles Ives. He always revered and admired Aaron Copland.

Then in 1976, the year of the American bicentennial, came an even stronger link. His old orchestra, the London Philharmonic, was due to make a bicentennial tour of the United States under its Principal Conductor, Bernard Haitink, and Arnold was asked for a new and celebratory work they could take across the Atlantic. He responded with a fifteen-minute firework display, the Philharmonic Concerto, op. 120. The commission, and the thought of 1776, lifted his depression.

> The middle of the eighteenth century seems to me to have been one of the most stimulating and interesting times in human history. The music, literature and the arts in general, particularly that of architecture, flourished with unsurpassed splendour. What, however, has such great significance for us in the present day are the great eighteenth century struggles for freedom amongst subject

> peoples. These of course found their peak with the American War of Independence of 1776. This piece has no quotations from war songs. It celebrates this great event with as much brilliance as I am able to muster, in what to me is the glorious sound of a symphony orchestra.[15]

For once Arnold's comment can be taken at face value. The Philharmonic Concerto, op. 120, is indeed a celebratory work, full of life-enhancing vitality. The Intrada with its ingenious twelve-note theme is one of Arnold's noisiest movements ever, the central Aria offers solos to each section of the orchestra in rotation, while the theme of the final Chacony, clustered tightly round the six semitones either side of the note E flat, is a rumbustious and virtuoso piece that proceeds at a blistering pace, even though it manages at one moment to embrace the sardonic flavour of a Viennese waltz. For all the advance in his musical confidence and language, Arnold's Philharmonic Concerto shares much of the *joie de vivre* that was evident in some of his more flamboyant earlier scores – and which he found characteristic of the American Dream.

The epilogue to Arnold's Irish years is provided by a work that he began in Dublin, but only completed back in London after his suicide attempt: 'The Symphony is a very Irish piece. I was longing to get back to Ireland, but I didn't want to go. Somehow these things are contradictory.'[16]

This is the Eighth Symphony, op. 124, which has links both with America and Ireland. It was commissioned by an American charitable trust, the Rustam K. Kermani Foundation[17], and first performed in the fine-sounding hall at Albany in New York State by the Albany Symphony Orchestra. And it also has an unexpected link to one of Arnold's final film scores, *The Reckoning*.

The film is based on Patrick Hall's novel *The Harp that Once*, which deals with a crisis in the life of a lapsed Irishman who has settled successfully but uneasily into the life of a London businessman. A telephone call from a man named Donnelly tells him his father is dying. Michael Marler therefore returns to the working-class Irish family he would far rather have forgotten, to discover that his father has died from a heart attack after a pub brawl. The identity of the man responsible is known to Michael Marler's ex-friends and acquaintances, who want to know what action the London turncoat (as they see him) is going to take in reply. Their code demands repayment in kind. The challenge to Marler is to his divided allegiances, and is also a test of his courage under all kinds of unfamiliar pressures.

The novel does not shirk the violence underlying these tensions. Nor did the film. It is clearly possible to find in both book and film strong pre-echoes of the conflicts that erupted in the troubles that plague Ireland to this day. Arnold's principal musical theme for the film was a catchy, march-like tune that lent itself to a variety of guises, including the film's more aggressive moments. Taking his cue from Patrick Hall's title, he modelled the march on the traditional Irish tune of the same name, whose accompanying words speak of Ireland's pride and freedom. Challenged, once, as to whether this might even be a covert message of support for the IRA, Arnold quickly denied it[18] – but his Irish sympathies were strong, and the choice of the tune could certainly be seen as a form of political gesture, albeit in a much lower key.

The incorporation of the selfsame melody, unaltered, into his Eighth Symphony therefore has implications along the lines of his earlier political gesture in the Fourth Symphony, where the use of Caribbean percussion was in part intended as an anti-racist statement. By any reckoning, it is a fine work and some – such as John Amis[19] – make out a strong case for the Eighth as Malcolm Arnold's masterpiece.

The thinking behind such an assertion has to do with its relative balance and proportion, coming after the tumult that prevails through much of the Seventh. The Eighth is a much less desolate proposition, more classically balanced. From that point of view it perhaps occupies a similar position to Beethoven's Eighth within his canonical nine. Perhaps it is Arnold's *Tempest* after his *King Lear*. The pattern of tension and resolution is made clear by the presence of the Irish tune inherited from the film *The Reckoning*. Its regular shape and fife-and-drum rhythm – it is first announced on Arnold's favourite piccolo – haunt the entire movement, as it reappears not only in an ingenious variety of guises, but balances the flailing discords that are its counterpart: for instance, screaming high woodwind, brass fanfares, pounding timpani at the opening. The whole movement is more transparent than its equivalent in the Seventh Symphony, because the textures have to let the tune through. Solos predominate, even for the timpani, and there is more than an echo of Shostakovich – a side-drum ostinato at one point recalls the *Leningrad* Symphony. There are novelties of texture in the slow movement too. Though it is marked andantino, the music is far from superficial. Recalling the memorial origin of the American commission, it is if anything elegiac in tone. The artful simplicity of its threnody, with the strings in their lowest registers, is soon accompanied by bitonal solos on horn and oboe. The bitonality, though, is poignant rather than aggressive as in the first movement.

A surprise erupts in the finale. It whirls back to the world of Arnold's Scottish Dances of a quarter of a century earlier, in an uninhibited three-four vivace demanding the highest degree of virtuosity. It is almost a concerto for orchestra. Perhaps the most hair-raising moment is the sound of the dance on four horns in unison, doubled by clarinets and all playing at maximum possible volume. The ending is a resounding cadence on D major. How much of an answer to the preceding two movements is this orchestral riot? It is certainly an assertion of brazen high spirits and major-key confidence, brushing aside confusion and uncertainty. If the previous two movements had conveyed anything like the desperation, even despair, of the Seventh Symphony, Arnold's answer might have been felt as simplistic. But they do not; and the rightness of his conclusion is not in doubt. And so, ironically, the music which preceded the composer's total collapse ends on a note of optimism and musical health.

When this Eighth Symphony was first performed in Albany, in the United States which Arnold had come to love, it was slow to gain acceptance. At home, too, it took its time. The first British performance had to wait a further two years until 1981, when his old ally Sir Charles Groves programmed it during a visit to the

BBC Northern Symphony Orchestra. Arnold, though, was particularly fond of one description of it that he heard in the United States: there, the symphony was described as a *flop d'estime*.[20]

7 : The Return of Odysseus

or *The Angry Silence*

'The critics have got to live – but for Christ's sake why don't they let me live too?'

The five years that Malcolm and Isobel Arnold spent in Ireland thus ended in disaster and near-tragedy. It was obvious to both sides that the marriage was over. Unwilling to suffer any longer Isobel left him, returning to England and taking Edward with her and – after Arnold had followed them across the Irish Sea – obtaining a court order shutting him out of their lives. They were divorced the same year. He took a flat in Holmfield Court, in the Belsize Park area of London, by chance not very far away from where he had stayed after the break-up of his first marriage to Sheila Nicholson. He continued to drink heavily, and it told both against his friendships and his desire to be involved in practical music-making. In April 1979 he agreed to be involved in an EMI recording of his two Flute Concertos with Richard Adeney that was eventually directed by Ronald Thomas, the Bournemouth Sinfonietta's Australian leader.

> Malcolm was to have conducted, but he had a psychotic breakdown just before the recording, which, although it was a tragedy, started with dreadful comedy. He was staying in Bournemouth at the grandest of Grand Hotels and during dinner, in front of the most respectable room-full of blue-rinse ladies, he stood up and shouted, 'You old hags, this place is boring'. He then

> left his table, climbed on to the closed lid of the grand piano, stripped entirely naked from the waist down and did a dance to the hotel's background music. He was hurried off to bed, but woke everyone in the middle of the night by banging the dinner gong and shouting for breakfast. He was in hospital for some time after that.[1]

History began to repeat itself. Out of hospital and back in Holmfield Court, almost out of habit and for want of anything better to do, he worked on a commission he felt unable to refuse, both for reasons of friendship, and because it brought into play all kinds of echoes from his brass-playing past. Once again, life and music intermingled: 'It was a sombre piece because I was entirely on my own. I was within a few minutes' walking distance from my wife and son. I had bought myself a flat, but I was just alone and I never saw them except when I was out shopping. As I say, it is a sombre piece.'[2]

This dark reference is to the only substantial piece of music, other than the Eighth Symphony, that Malcolm Arnold wrote between 1978 and 1986, the year he was finally to settle in Norfolk. The work in question is another symphony, not part of the numerical canon, conceived as an occasional piece but much more than even a *succès d'estime*, especially in America, where it has been widely taken up. This is the Symphony for Brass, op. 123, written for another trumpeter, Philip Jones, as a fiftieth birthday present and scored for a configuration of ten instruments: five trumpets including piccolo trumpet, three trombones, horn and tuba. Arnold knew that it presented some kind of zenith and that expectations would be high. This was, after all, a trumpeter-turned-composer writing for the ultimate brass combination, a symphonic brass ensemble.

It was, however, a miracle that the Symphony for Brass was finished at all. His difficulty in starting the piece greatly worried his friends, Philip Jones among them. In her history of the Philip Jones Brass Ensemble,[3] Donna McDonald records that the composer's 'inability to start the Symphony only deepened his gloom. To try to help him, the Joneses invited him to their home, and while Ursula plied him with cakes, Philip played him the recording of Elgar Howarth's arrangement for the group of Mussorgsky's *Pictures at an Exhibition*, so he could appreciate the capabilities of the Ensemble.'

She also feels that some of this despondency crept into the music itself, finding the piece darker in tone than much of his earlier music and describing it as 'obscure'. Arnold's music has seldom been called that! Yet, half thinking it was unlikely to enjoy an extended after-life, Arnold deliberately made it 'fiendishly difficult'.[4]

The world this grim masterwork inhabits is light-years away from the conventional formulae of the brass-band world, from his own brilliant earlier Brass Quintet no. 1 and from his various concertos for brass instruments. Into it went nearly sixty years' worth of love for sounding brass; his vast experience of brass sonorities, techniques and capabilities is audible on every page. All this is clear from the outset: the Symphony begins with long-held triads on the trumpets, while horn and tuba, two octaves apart, intone a dark, growling theme full of sombre possibilities and in the work's hard-fought passage from dark to light they are to be amply realised. In the development Arnold makes a bold formal experiment within his sonata shape, sliding cunningly into a racing nine-eight vivace, in which furious skirling semiquavers drive the music relentlessly forward. The return to the dark music of the opening has a powerfully sobering effect and, after the minor key, the major third in the final chord – an old-fashioned *tierce de Picardie* – is a welcome ray of sunlight.

Then comes an Intermezzo, gentle, mostly quiet, much of it in two-part counterpoint, with plenty of solos – and duets. Arnold could by now have heard Benjamin Britten's Third String Quartet; its deeply original first movement is called Duets, and is full of the same kind of intricate instrumental interplay. In particular, in Arnold's Symphony a long duet between tuba and bass trombone, unpromising on paper, is handled in masterly fashion, while the movement's epilogue, requiring mutes, is music of poignancy and resignation. The music of the following andante con moto scatters stillness to the winds, however, and it is clearly twelve-note in inspiration. Later a march-like recitative, marked fortissimo, is contrasted with quiet lyrical solos for horn and trombone. The finale underlines the sincerity of Arnold's symphonic aspirations in the work, in that (unlike the Brass Quintet, for example, where the finale merely entertains) it makes a serious attempt at resolving previous arguments. The chosen means is a fearsomely difficult double fugue, with some original structural features – there is a lengthy lyrical respite, until the return of the fugue, pp and muted, leads straight into a sonorous major-key coda. The horn and tuba theme of the first movement reappears and in this way Arnold boldly allies an overall cyclical shape to his fugal resolution. The device has many precedents, notably in the highly experimental opus 20 quartets of his admired Haydn: unlike a somewhat less effective fugue in his early Organ Concerto, his use of fugue in the Symphony for Brass is at once spontaneous and a vigorous reassertion of Arnold's awareness of himself as a descendant of the great classical tradition.

Whatever the awkwardnesses surrounding the birth of the Symphony for Brass, Philip Jones was delighted with the outcome, and his Ensemble went on to make a magnificent-sounding recording of a work unlikely to prove overwhelmingly popular but destined to remain one of the Everests of brass literature.

After the two 1978 symphonies, the work for brass and then no. 8, for nearly eight years there was silence, broken only by the miniature-length Trumpet Concerto of 1982. This was a time of depression, self-doubt, loneliness and further breakdown – the lowest ebb in all Malcolm Arnold's composing life. The most famous of musical silences is the thirty years at the end of Sibelius's life in Finland. But that was the silence of retirement. Arnold's silence was something else.

The grip of alcohol was as powerful as ever. In 1981, after over a year of steadily worsening circumstances, he spent some months being dried out at a recuperation establishment called St Andrew's near his home town of Northampton. The irony of the hospital's location was not lost on the composer of *John Clare Cantata*. St Andrew's looked rather like a stately home set in rolling parkland; and it had once had its own dairy. But it was built as an asylum and John Clare, the mad poet from Arnold's county of Northamptonshire, was a patient there for the latter years of his life. The early years of the nineteenth century were more enlightened than many other periods in their treatment of the mentally ill: it was as much concerned with moral therapy as with physical restraint and John Clare – like Malcolm Arnold – had a private room and considerable freedom. The fact remained that poet and composer each found himself a patient in St Andrew's for powerful and painful reasons, to do with illness and breakdown.

The loyalty of Arnold's friends at this time was sorely tested. Charles Groves did not forget him. Sally Cavender from his publishers made uncomfortable visits. Richard Adeney, witnessing the decline in his creativity and upset at his pathetic condition, wondered if it was the result of a lobotomy. Others simply forgot his existence.

When he was discharged from St Andrew's, Arnold's troubles continued. The local Social Services by now had him on their register; and this was indirectly to cause him further misfortune. His social worker was a woman called Sally Charlton, whose husband Brian was an ex-policeman. When Arnold left St Andrew's the Charltons offered him a room in their home. At first all was well. Then Sally Charlton died, Brian Charlton got married again to an Irish girl and matters deteriorated. Arnold's presence became an intrusion. Among the difficulties, the couple were still responsible for administering his medication and Arnold was forced into a dependency not of his choosing.

And yet he could be eminently rational and continued to give the occasional interview. Michael Oliver visited him in St Andrew's for BBC Radio 3 in 1981, on his sixtieth birthday, and found him interested in many things: keen to talk about his admiration for the Viennese serialist Anton Webern and expressing an enthusiasm for Peter Maxwell Davies. But performances and his reputation were at a low ebb. The BBC, asked by one of its producers[5] if a cycle of the symphonies could be organised for the same occasion, declined. Recordings dropped to nil. His publishers, Faber Music, became deeply worried. Alan Poulton, who briefly became his business manager after first producing an admirable catalogue of his music, lost the composer's confidence and they parted company. The death of his old friend William Walton in March 1983 increased his depression.

Arnold became increasingly difficult to deal with, sometimes irrational and often aggressive in conversation even to those who had been staunch allies. The generous wit could be, as in the past, malicious but was seldom tempered by his former kindness. He was dependent on medication for any degree of stability. His business affairs, and particularly the copyright and performance revenues, were taken from his hands and put into those of the Court of Protection and some of the early decisions caused him much anger. Later Emrys Lloyd-Roberts (an official of the Court who some years on became the dedicatee of the Welsh Dances) inherited the brief; he proved to be more sympathetic and worked to sort out the worst of the confusion. When Arnold came to Norfolk his doctors gave him two years to live and predicted he would never compose again.

Malcolm Arnold is certainly not alone among creative artists in having suffered thus. His creativity was almost destroyed; and when he came out on the other side, it was undeniably affected – for the worse, claimed his critics. Many of them would have known nothing of the domestic and psychological background; others would have said that it was irrelevant anyway. The life of the creative artist is by its very nature intensely demanding; the best ceaselessly look inwards, subjecting themselves to extremes that those who do not live life on the same exalted plane can only guess at. There is a case for seeing the artist's life from the artist's point of view. In Malcolm Arnold's case, there was one aspect of his life as an artist which in his own view as well as that of his second wife Isobel[5] had contributed substantially to his downfall.

Within the matrix of urges and motivations, influences and pressures from both within and without that make up the creative personality of any worthwhile artist, there is one particular area where Malcolm Arnold had become almost pathologically sensitive. Was his hatred of the musical press, which by the end of the Seventies had grown into something of an obsession, justified? Was it a contributory factor in his descent to the depths? Some of the phraseology which greeted his symphonies – the works by which he himself set most store – was vitriolic. His excellent memory retained many notices word for word.

Over the initials J. W., the *Daily Telegraph* of 3 December 1957 reviewed the Third Symphony and wrote of Arnold's 'repetitive and conventional gestures'. The *Observer* of 4 November 1960 condescended to find some 'attractive material' in the first movement of the Fourth Symphony, but the approval was short-lived. 'The slow movement is a failure. Its material is undistinguished, and here again a lack of momentum is not disguised by resort to the facile climaxes of routine film music.' And later, 'Mr Arnold shows no ability to develop the initial idea . . . finally he throws in the sponge with the dreariest clichés of popular music.' William Mann, reviewing the Seventh Symphony in *The Times*, on 6 May 1974, found the music 'not only bewildering but . . . verbose and unprofitable. Brooding evidently has an adverse effect on Malcolm Arnold.' The long-delayed première of the Ninth Symphony was greeted with similar incomprehension by David Fanning in the *Independent* of 22 January 1992: 'The ostensibly fast opening movement and its moderately paced successor often sound like mere accompaniments to some more interesting but suppressed music . . . Arnold's pared-down style seems to go hand in hand with slackness rather than concentration.'

The chorus of recrimination never really abated. Notoriously, the Fifth Symphony provoked the critic in *The Times* to write about 'a creative personality in an advanced state of disintegration', and Jeremy Noble to speak of 'a jolly neo-Romantic confection'. Writing about the Second String Quartet, Peter Stadlen in the *Daily Telegraph* claimed that Arnold 'excels in ivory-tower conservatism'. *The Times* wrote of the Cello Concerto that it contained 'rudimentary forms filled with scraps of tune, and a slow-moving orchestral line articulated with grotesque out-of-scale crashes'. In February 1990 Geoffrey Thomason in the

Guardian wrote brutally that 'Arnold has suddenly embraced minimalism, and the cause seems to be sheer lack of imagination'.

Hans Keller, who had written sympathetically on Malcolm Arnold in the early Fifties, wrote a devastating analysis of the possible damage inflicted by insensitive criticism – which he labelled a 'phoney profession'. Damage, he asserted, was inflicted on all parties, artist, public, and the critic himself. But it is the artist who suffers most: 'professing to have discovered artistic deficiencies, [the critic] will as often as not invent them and thus saddle the artist with the experience of having been libelled without having any chance of redress – a profound human problem if ever there was one.'[6] Keller's two chosen examples were Schoenberg and Benjamin Britten; Malcolm Arnold could easily have made a third.

What was distressing was the intemperance of critical language and the fact that the attacks seemed to be almost personal. Desmond Shawe-Taylor, the critic of the *Sunday Times*, let rip indiscriminately in his column of 6 November 1960. Having patronised Arnold's earlier music as 'charming . . . lightweight . . . good-humoured', the tone of superiority grew as the critic contemplated a new work. 'Never an inhibited man, Mr Arnold has here shed the last rags of taste and discretion. Like a TV idol determined to exploit his personality for all it is worth, he has fairly played it up and piled it on. But the air that blew into the Festival Hall last Wednesday was no country breeze, but the stale scented air of the modern ballroom.' Consistent hostility also characterised the reviews of another critic, Max Harrison of *The Times*, and a notice that appeared just five days before Arnold's fiftieth birthday in October 1971 exceeded his previous efforts in the shameless hypocrisy of its opening. 'The nondescript quality of his compositions defies the greatest initial good will . . . The three movements of Arnold's Sinfonietta no. 2 are like pieces of cloth snipped at random from the same bolt . . . Involuntarily one asks, does Mr Arnold never stop to think? . . . The banality [of the closing vivace] really has no excuse.'

The ferocity of this attack even prompted a defence of Arnold from another critic, Gillian Widdicombe, then writing for the

Financial Times. 'Dog should not bark at dog, maybe; but then dogs should not be allowed out on 50th birthdays, particularly if they are either didactic or plain daft.' And in a notably generous retrospective, she went on to give a clear summary of the composer's career, enthusing in particular over the concertos – the Viola Concerto had been heard for the first time in London in the concert which had caused all the fuss.

As this last example shows, for all the savagery that Arnold was sometimes subjected to, there were nevertheless other voices to be heard, more sympathetic if less strident. Over many years, his old friend Hugo Cole, Edward Greenfield of the *Guardian*, and Colin Mason who wrote regularly for the *Daily Telegraph* were three critics who went out of their way to look below the surface of the music, trying to match what they heard to what they knew of the composer's intentions. Occasionally, others joined in. R.L.H. in the *Guardian* of 5 July 1961, reviewing the Fifth Symphony at Cheltenham, said that 'Arnold displays yet again his seemingly inexhaustible melodic invention and imaginative resource' – and evidently grasped the nature of the symphony's conflicting polarities, writing of the 'unrest that moves between the opposing centres, one of a sweet, sentimental nostalgia, and the other a gritty, almost cynical defiance'. Likewise, it is an anonymous reviewer in *The Times* of 3 November 1960 who, in one of the more perceptive notices the composer received, sees instantly what the Fourth Symphony is driving at, underlining 'the inspiration, though not the influence, of Mahler', recognising its Mahlerian aspirations and all-embracing musical vocabulary, and defining the intended audience: 'the symphony is clearly addressed to the man in the street outside: bourgeois, unsophisticated, musically Philistine perhaps, but a person of spirit, faced like any of us with the problem of living in a world over whose uncertain destinies he has no control. Arnold puts the issues forward in this man's musical language, and brings them to a head.'

For every insight such as this, there were howls of derision in far greater number. Human nature being what it is, Arnold felt the pain of rejection far more sharply than the balm of acclamation. From initial indifference and resignation, his dislike and mistrust of the critics began to assume a pathological quality. Any creative artist needs to feel a measure of acceptance and understanding, or his entire *raison d'écrire* is undermined. Arnold was deeply wounded by press attitudes to his work. Yet it is important to distinguish between Arnold's feelings about his treatment at the hands of the press, and about his acceptability to the musical public at large. Looking back at the time of his sixty-fifth birthday,[7] he was adamant that he had nothing to reproach the public for, and bore no grudge. On the contrary, 'the composer is the servant of the public'.

On the whole, Arnold shared Beecham's view, that musicians should be doers not sayers. The boot had even on one occasion been on the other foot: on 2 November 1958 Malcolm Arnold wrote a column for the *Sunday Times*, deputising for Ernest Newman. He used the allotted space to mount a fierce attack on the commercialisation of London musical life, the narrow-mindedness and timidity of promoters, conductors and soloists, and the underpayment of orchestral musicians generally. Eventually, though, his patience ran out. He wrote a bitter piece attacking the critical trade as it had been practised throughout musical history, and damning the majority of its current exponents as ignorant amateurs. The article, headed 'Don't shoot the pianist' after a then popular Truffaut film, is reprinted at the back of this biography, and if there is more than a touch of self-pity about it, it is abundantly obvious that Malcolm Arnold had been goaded past endurance, to the point where he was unable to suffer any more in silence. Conceivably, at some deeper level of cause and effect, critical hostility was one of the triggers behind his retreats to Cornwall and then to Ireland and a further destabilising factor in a personality already dangerously prone to huge swings between elation and gloom.

Arnold's breakdown, with its resulting spell in St Andrew's and almost total musical silence for nearly eight years, evidently had a lifetime of causes: physical and mental, social and psychological, medical and intellectual. There had been no hint of instability in his parents' generation. But it had been suspected in his sister Ruth, expelled from the Slade, who then developed an interest in spiritualism, and in his eldest brother, whose business misfortunes had caused him to take his own life. And in Ireland Malcolm Arnold had made a second violent assault on himself to follow his wartime attempt. Not surprisingly, there was now also a nagging fear that some of this instability might be part of his son Edward's genetic inheritance. No one wanted to put labels on Malcolm Arnold's condition, but within it there were elements of manic depression, alcoholism, possibly even schizophrenia.

This last was a term often used loosely and ill-advisedly, as it had been about Malcolm Arnold himself, about the time of the Army escapade. His behaviour seemed to some to fit the pattern uncomfortably. Sufferers can be in remission for months at a time, before an episode occurs when least expected and in a way apparently calculated to cause maximum disruption. R. D. Laing's theory that schizophrenia was a reaction to intolerable social pressures, widely accepted in the Sixties, is by now discredited – though Arnold's case might in some measure seem to confirm it. Instead, like autism, schizophrenia is now assumed to be caused by a chemical imbalance in the brain. Emotions, perceptions and memories become, in the worst cases, impossibly confused. Drugs can provide relief, but not a cure.

Yet Malcolm Arnold's memory for events and people, incidents and occasions, remained robust and exact, even when he was displaying those more negative symptoms – withdrawal, silence, self-neglect – that often overlap with those of severe depression. He never lost his pride in his appearance. Medication in the form of dopamine blockers, however, became a permanent necessity. Arnold suffered the inevitable side-effects – not just the appearance of being half asleep much of the time, but also involuntary nervous movements of the face. He was a disconcertingly unpredictable companion, whose occasional good days were sometimes offset by bad ones. In such confusion, even despair, music inevitably took a back seat.

8 : Solitaire

or *The Inn of the Sixth Happiness*

'I'm Malcolm Arnold now –
he just writes the music.'

On 28 May 1984, Malcolm Arnold was collected from the Tower Hotel in his home town of Northampton by Anthony Day, who remembers meeting 'a pitiful, timorous creature' wholly unable to fend for himself. Two years later, talking about his Ninth Symphony which he completed in 1986, Malcolm Arnold spoke tersely of the years that had passed since his previous symphony, confessing that he had 'been through hell'.[1] Hell appeared in retrospect to consist largely of doctors and lawyers, agents and publishers, alcohol and pills. When, eventually, he parted company with the Charltons and the pub in Northampton where they lived, he left behind most of the possessions he had with him in the Crown & Cushion, including a random assortment of papers and manuscripts, and even more painfully, the insignia of his CBE. All he managed to retain at this new climacteric in his life was, symbolically, the writing desk at which much of his music had been composed and the much-prized clavichord which Thomas Goff had built for him nearly forty years earlier, the same instrument on which he had once played jazz in Richmond with Julian Bream.

The original intention behind Anthony Day's involvement was to see the composer through some sort of rehabilitation period;

he was to care for him, run the home and stabilise Arnold's life. But in the early stages Day found himself acting more as a kind of nurse-cum-guardian, while Arnold rapidly became reliant on his companion simply to get him through the daily routine. The relationship became permanent, changing and developing as the years went by, until from the outside it looked like a form of mutual dependence with complex factors at work on both sides.

The initial intermediary, between the two men responsible for suggesting the original arrangement, was Mike Purton, then a television producer with BBC East based in Norwich. Purton had wanted to make a film about the composer, discovered where he was and had been to see him. Back in his home village in Norfolk, Purton had at about the same time come to know Anthony Day, a trained secretary, chef and hairdresser but currently at something of a loose end. Day's patron and employer for the previous four and a half years had been a millionaire businessman, Robert Strauss who, like Day, was gay. After Strauss's death from a brain tumour Day, much affected, had for a time found a job on the cruise liner *Queen Elizabeth II*; but he was now back in Norfolk with his parents who lived next door to Mike Purton. The suggestion that Day should look after Malcolm Arnold for a while was a timely one, particularly as Norfolk seemed the best place for this, with several of his family members on hand, able to provide any further necessary support. It also seemed imperative to remove the composer from the dark shadow of Northampton.

And so Malcolm Arnold moved to Norfolk, initially to a charming rented cottage in the village of Wymondham, which the two men had found on one of their daily excursions. These trips had been recommended by the doctors for their therapeutic value; with the additional suggestion that the composer be encouraged to listen to tapes of his own music. Arnold remembered that he had links with the county in the shape of his great-grandfather Thomas Hawes, who was for twenty-five years Rector of Burgh Castle, near Great Yarmouth, and was buried in the churchyard there. Many years earlier Arnold had even made a sentimental journey to see the place. Encountering the then incumbent, Arnold told him of his ancestor. 'Apart from being buried here, I don't think he did much else for the place,' was the comment. Arnold took some delight in pointing out that Thomas Hawes had also written two hymns that were printed in the first edition of *Hymns Ancient and Modern* – while conceding that they had dated more than most.

Anthony Day also had Norfolk roots and they were even stronger than those of his charge. He had been born and brought up in the county, still spoke with a trace of its flat accent, could recall rural Norfolk life in the early Fifties and the city of Norwich before it had become prettified as a heritage site. He was much attracted by the fenland landscapes and as a child had been on boating holidays on the Norfolk Broads. Such antecedents helped bind the two men together, for the composer could recall[1] his grandfather hiring a cruiser for the whole Arnold family and that there had even been a piano on board. Later he had played in Norwich with the London Philharmonic, at concerts in the old Regal Cinema conducted by Constant Lambert or the Cathedral organist Heathcote Statham. This common ground, modest as it was, gave the initially tentative relationship some tangible footing on which to gain a hold.

This basis was certainly necessary. Although Robert Strauss had introduced him to ballet, and to the music of Mozart and Beethoven and a few others, Anthony Day was candid about his lack of knowledge of music and he had certainly never heard a note of Malcolm Arnold's. To all outward appearances, the longer the relationship continued and the stronger it became, the less likely it seemed. At the start, the first requirement was largely one of organising the daily round, as well as looking after appointments and travel arrangements and trying to keep Arnold away from drink. There were frequent consultations with doctors and psychiatrists to be attended. Then, gradually, Anthony Day grew to know and admire much of Arnold's music, while the composer gradually felt willing and able to attend the occasional concert where a piece of his was being performed; only locally at first and always with Day in attendance. Commissions, conducting engagements and even interviews were still, for the moment, impossibilities. Musical and financial matters were dealt with, as they had been before his departure from Northampton, far away in London by a combination of lawyers at the Court of Protection, publishers and eventually, a year after Day's arrival on the scene, by a new figure who styled herself Malcolm Arnold's 'personal representative', but who soon became an essential part of his life.

Georgina Ivor was a former artists' agent who had left Harold Holt's to have a family and, after the trauma of a divorce, was seeking to find her way back into the musical world and was therefore admirably qualified to help in many respects. Recommended to the composer initially by his publishers, the resourceful and persistent Ms Ivor's primary function was that of securing performances, which would supply much-needed royalty income for the composer. Although she was able to identify the performers and promoters most likely to respond to Arnold's music, by her own account she was sometimes disheartened, working alone out of her South London office for a composer who was prone, even on good days, to be difficult and from whom, given his physical and mental state, not much could be expected by way of involvement, certainly until his condition improved. She did not give up, however, and slowly performances, recordings and broadcasts of Arnold's music all began to pick up.

The process started locally in Norfolk. Amateur and educational groups, learning of Malcolm Arnold's presence nearby, plucked up the courage to programme his music and to invite him to performances and rehearsals, sometimes even to conduct. Wymondham College, just a mile or two from his new home, was quick to seize the opportunity, as was the County Youth Orchestra. The Festivals at King's Lynn and in Norwich itself began to show an interest. Such activity, relatively undemanding as far as Arnold was concerned, was congenial, even therapeutic. London, however, was still out of the question.

Anthony Day also began quietly to encourage Arnold to try to write music again, more as therapy than with any real hope of significant achievement. It seemed a logical suggestion to make; particularly to a man whose self-respect had apparently been largely dependent on his art. Yet, since the exiguous Trumpet Concerto of February 1982, Arnold had not written a note. The paralysis of creative mind and will that had almost entirely overtaken him after 1979 still had him in its grip.

It was another woman who contributed to keeping Arnold's compositional flame alight, after even the composer himself thought he had shot his bolt, and who stayed loyal to the three separate works he wrote for her in the space of four years. The Danish recorder virtuoso Michala Petri first came to musical attention as a child prodigy, tackling not only the entire baroque repertory for her instrument, but also modern recorder classics such as Berio's *Gesti* and Shinohara's *Fragmente* with extraordinary aplomb. Petri had emerged from adolescence and her mother's careful tutelage as a mature and beautiful artist with her own decided musical convictions. Arnold happened to watch a television programme on which she appeared in November 1985 and soon afterwards, as she was appearing at a concert at Wingfield College over the border in Suffolk, Anthony Day drove him to hear it. Composer and performer met and the suggestion was made that she come to Wymondham the next day, as she had no engagement. She did, they talked and, already familiar with Arnold's very early Recorder Sonatina, she asked him to write her a new piece, without accompaniment this time, which she could take with her on her frequent tours. Arnold agreed, though still at a low ebb. It was not until the following June that he set pen to paper. Thirteen months after that, in July 1987, Michala Petri played the Fantasy for solo descant recorder for the first time at a recital in Beccles Church in Suffolk. She fell in love with it, took it into her repertoire, promised to programme it regularly, fulfilled her promise and made the definitive recording.

The work offered fresh evidence that Arnold's language had changed subtly. As the Ninth Symphony was also soon to show, his music was more elusive, more compressed than before, with bare textures and long angular melodic lines unsupported by an accompaniment. With this piece for Michala Petri, and one that was to follow later in the year for Julian Lloyd Webber, Arnold now returned increasingly to a form that had preoccupied him in the Sixties, the solo instrumental Fantasy. It held many attractions. For one thing, the relative freedom of the form was undemanding. As the name implies, the Fantasy imposes almost no restrictions except those of the instrument in question. Arnold was thus content to build on what he had achieved in his earlier successful examples, both the shorter pieces such as the haunting Fantasy for Tuba, or multi-sectioned works such as the solo Fantasies he had once penned for Julian Bream or Osian Ellis.

Yet, though Georgina Ivor and Michala Petri were key figures in the revival of Malcolm Arnold's fortunes, women seemed (after a brief relationship begun in Northampton and terminated early in 1986) largely excluded from the composer's circle. Prone in the past to an unthinking male chauvinism, and embittered latterly by the failure of his two marriages, he retained a deep-seated suspicion of the female sex that was compounded further by his unstable condition. Even with medication he was still uncomfortably prone to acts of spontaneous verbal aggression. Georgina Ivor, and also Sally Cavender from his long-time publishers Faber Music, suffered occasional hurt as a result, even while staying loyal to the man and his music and recognising that he could also, on good days, charm and delight. This aggression was not confined to women. Old friends generally found that he was not the person they had known. Still moody and unforthcoming, he could often appear to be in a complete daze, only to snap out of it with a wounding remark. Interviewers were frequently caught off guard. On public occasions an apparent demonstration of good behaviour might be accompanied by uncontrolled remarks from the side of the mouth that were not always pleasant to hear. Within the confines of their home in Wymondham, and later at Attleborough where they moved in 1988, Anthony Day was to suffer more than most. And yet, on many other occasions when no clouds darkened the sky and he felt unthreatened by life, Malcolm Arnold could still be the sunniest and most agreeable of companions, as Day in particular was also finding.

It had been over two years from the first meeting between Day and Arnold before the latter wrote any music at all, starting with the Recorder Fantasy; but when he finally took up his pen again, it seemed briefly, in the autumn of 1986, as if a floodgate had been opened and a torrent unleashed. Eventually, after smaller beginnings, came a Ninth Symphony, a musical encapsulation of all he had lived through. In the past, to be sure, Arnold had usually had a symphony brewing continuously, even though there could sometimes be gaps of a number of years. Finishing one symphony appeared to release his subconscious mind to brood on the next. Given the extraordinary speed with which the Ninth eventually emerged into the daylight, it is a fair assumption that it had taken a similar path to that of its predecessors – that is, a prolonged, unwritten gestation, the actual birth and delivery being much delayed by the traumas of Arnold's private life.

The Ninth had in fact had a tortuous earlier history, in which the BBC played a not insignificant part. The idea, and the Ninth's link with Manchester where it was eventually premièred, went back to before the Eighth Symphony of 1979, when David Ellis, then the BBC's Head of Music North, asked the composer as they were driving back across the Pennines after he had conducted a concert with the BBC Northern Symphony Orchestra if he would write his next symphony for them. Arnold agreed, but explained that no. 8 was already promised to a Foundation – and orchestra – in the United States. Ellis therefore arranged for the Ninth to be commissioned as one of the BBC's contributions to European Music Year, planned for 1985. Then came the long delay occasioned by the composer's breakdown and period of ill-health. Despite the long lead-time, the symphony was not ready even for European Music Year; and London, which had not been properly consulted by Manchester in the first place and now saw both the deadline and an important occasion missed, withdrew the promise of funding.

When the symphony was eventually completed on 5 September 1986, embarrassment ensued, as first the BBC – where there had been a change of personnel both in Manchester and in London – and Arnold's then publisher, Faber Music, took fright at the score, which was radically different from the composer's previous symphonies. The BBC's original interest was not renewed. The publishers were concerned at what looked like the sheer emptiness of the score – metaphorically and literally in its many empty lines. And on the page it bore an unmistakable note of finality about it – particularly the long, slow finale.

If that note of finality was indeed present in the symphony – a form which Arnold on more than one occasion said he regarded as the highest form of musical composition – then it was intentional. He himself had consciously or unconsciously sensed that, whatever his circumstances or the state of his health, he was unlikely to have the strength or motivation to write a Tenth. The Ninth therefore assumed an enormous symbolic importance for him; which made his publishers' reservations, and the difficulties Georgina Ivor began to experience in getting it accepted for performance, at first exasperating and eventually the source of much bitterness on the composer's part. The eventual première of the symphony took place more than five years after its completion, in Manchester in 1992.

At the time it was finished in September 1986, however, it was evidently a great purging of all that had been contained within him, musically, since 1979. If his own claim is taken at face value, that the Ninth Symphony was composed in eighteen days, working for fifteen hours each day with barely a pause for a cup of coffee, it means only that this was the period it took Arnold to get it down on paper. He had in earlier times claimed not only that he always had a symphony at the back of his mind, but even that he conceived and memorised 'entire works in fully orchestrated form before ever putting pen to paper'[2] and the Ninth conformed to this pattern. He knew he must write it, out of internal and external compulsion. The date it was begun, though, was perhaps significant. The twelfth of August 1986 was Anthony Day's birthday.

The writing of the symphony evidently marked some turning-point – though quite what corner had been turned was not clear even to those who were closest to him at this time. Anthony Day continued to see to his daily needs and their relationship had evidently begun to change, as the fact of the symphony's dedication to him made clear.

Dependency of the kind that Arnold was showing soon put his companion in the way of shouldering greater responsibilities than before. He had already helped with the work of the Court of Protection and after several attempts to have Arnold released from its jurisdiction, which were ultimately successful, Arnold's finances were back on a reasonably secure footing. Eventually Anthony Day was even able to share some of Georgina Ivor's work on the musical side, including dealings with Arnold's publishers. Increasingly composer and helper tended to be thought of as a pair; Arnold was seldom seen alone, as his public behaviour was still liable to be unpredictable and Day alone knew how to control it. This, coupled with Day's unconcealed homosexuality and with the intimacy occasioned by Arnold's requirement for physical assistance even in the bath, particularly after his heart attack in 1988, often led outsiders to conclude that the relationship was homosexual. In fact, Arnold did not share his companion's orientation.

Meanwhile a member of the new generation of talented young performers in Britain had also become interested in Arnold's music, with much the same consequences as had occurred in the case of Michala Petri. Julian Lloyd Webber gave Malcolm Arnold's Fantasy for Cello, op. 130, for the first time at the end of 1987 in the Wigmore Hall in London. Even more so than with the equivalent recorder work, the word for the piece can only be 'austere'. It is music stripped to its bare essentials. Once again Arnold fills the Fantasy form with a sequence of flowing but contrasted sections. The material is tightly linked thematically, the slow elegy of the opening page being transformed successively into a ghostly march, a sombre lento, and also a pizzicato scherzo section, before the opening is repeated note for note as a framework: in effect the Fantasy for Cello is thus a theme and variations with the theme repeated at the end. It was to prove one of the most personal of his late works.

Arnold's association with these two outstanding young artists, Michala Petri and Julian Lloyd Webber, followed much the same pattern as became typical in the heyday of Arnold's concertos in the Fifties and Sixties – reflecting the old joy of working with a particular instrumentalist, and incorporating something of his or her musical personality into the written notes, so that the finished work resembled a kind of musical portrait. With both Michala Petri and Julian Lloyd Webber, the portraits were to be extended over more than one work; in the case of the former it became a trilogy. A year after the Fantasy, to a commission from the county's arts association, Eastern Arts, Arnold wrote a concerto for recorder and classical-sized orchestra of strings with pairs of horns and oboes. Much of it is lyrical and bitter-sweet without being particularly memorable, though the middle movement is in his favourite chaconne form and the opening movement contains, in Arnold's own phrase, 'very special bits for Michala'.[3]

She played it for the first time in Suffolk in June 1988, but the composer was not present. Shortly before the première, at the end of April, he suffered a heart attack and was rushed to hospital in Norwich. It was not a severe one, though given his general medical condition it was serious enough and he was kept in hospital under observation. The setback was considerable. Looking after him, Anthony Day had to return to the role of nurse and to bear the brunt of Arnold's frustration and anger. Only a late holiday in the sunshine of North Africa relieved the strain of a difficult period, while for the rest of 1988 composition was once again out of the question.

Earlier in the year, before the heart attack, Arnold finished two further works in addition to the concerto for Michala Petri. One was a personal commission from an artist whom he much admired, the tenor Robert Tear. The singer was celebrating his fiftieth birthday and wanted a work to sing with string accompaniment. Arnold was flattered, but found it even more difficult to start than usual, having had no hand in the choice of texts. Robert Tear himself was responsible for the selection. He eventually gave his friend five of his favourite poems, by Samuel Johnson, Arnold's revered William Blake, the Japanese Chikamatsu Monzaemon and Emily Dickinson, as well as the anonymous 'Saint Jerome in his study'. Even so, Arnold's muse signally failed to ignite: the vocal line did little to enhance the words, while the string accompaniments were perfunctory. The resulting *Serenade* was a disappointment, and a harmful one, because a piece commissioned as a joyful celebration turned out to be hardly that. The musical world began to suspect that Malcolm Arnold wanted now to talk exclusively in the sombre, elliptical vein of the Cello Fantasy, that he was incapable of thinking except in miniature and that his old exuberance and warmth had deserted him for good.

When the Cello Concerto for Julian Lloyd Webber produced an equally unsympathetic reaction at the first performance by its dedicatee in March 1989, the impression seemed to be confirmed. Again part of the problem was that expectations were confounded. The concerto even bore a subtitle – 'Shakespearean' – and was given as part of the opening of a 'Shakespeare and Music' Festival. If in the public mind Arnold was a Falstaffian character, the resulting work could certainly not be so described. Rather than displaying any of the Elgarian wistfulness that the name Falstaff might evoke, it showed something of the same brittleness and anger that characterised a celebrated novel that appeared at about the same time, Kingsley Amis's *The Old Devils*. Energy is reserved for the short last movement, which is furious rather than ingratiating. Elsewhere in Arnold's Cello Concerto there is little by way of drama and the sombrely angular cantabile line of much of the cello part is sparsely, often enigmatically accompanied by the orchestra. Almost every melodic gesture in the whole concerto has a descending outline, which perhaps contributes to its ultimately depressed range of expression and contributed to its lukewarm critical reception.

If the critics were to a man either embarrassed or hostile, it was still possible to feel puzzlement rather than disappointment, and that the Cello Concerto's time might yet come. The times that it reflected were themselves, after all, hardly optimistic and Arnold was sufficiently aware of the reality of Margaret Thatcher's Britain to know that it was an often philistine place and that many of his countrymen were experiencing hardship in it. He continued to accept the occasional commission when those surrounding him felt that nothing too ambitious was being demanded and that musical work would provide him with some sort of vital stimulus. Thus 1989 finally saw the creation of a set of Four Welsh Dances to complement the earlier sets, though they scarcely made the impact of their English and Scottish predecessors of three decades earlier. The following year saw the completion of four new works, including two for young performers: an overture for the Norfolk Youth Orchestra, to which the composer characteristically attached the name of a prominent figure from Norfolk history, the sixteenth century rebel leader Robert Kett – he was a landowner from Arnold's adopted village of Wymondham who provoked a siege of Norwich by Royal forces and was executed in Norwich Castle in 1549: there is still a Kett's Hill in Norwich – and a third Little Suite, written for the Manx Youth Orchestra, whose conductor Alan Pickard helpfully sent over some Manx tunes which Arnold was able to incorporate into what he called his *Manx Suite*, op. 142.

Another commission seemed tailor-made to Arnold's old style and background. The fiftieth anniversary of the Battle of Britain was marked through the length and breadth of the country, the RAF Benevolent Fund launched a special appeal and Arnold, on the strength of his earlier involvement in the BBC TV series *War in the Air* and in Guy Hamilton's *Battle of Britain* film, was asked for a work for the inaugural appeal concert. The commission scarcely made the platform in time, for when the score was first produced it was found neither to be substantial enough, nor to fit the musical forces that had been assembled for what was, after all, to be a Royal occasion. A certain amount of frantic writing and copying saved the day – but only just. The battle sequence which it contains is effective enough, but is repeated once too often and there is a shortage of contrasting material. Disappointment again ensued and the Central Band of the RAF did not take Arnold's *Flourish for a Battle* into their regular repertoire.

There remained only the stimulus of Michala Petri's recorder-playing to provide musical encouragement. In good time for their centenary season, the Carnegie Hall Corporation in New York asked Arnold for a work to be premièred in the small hall of that famous auditorium. Towards the end of 1990 he completed a short piece which effectively combined elements of his previous two works for her, the Fantasy and Concerto. The new piece was called Fantasy for Recorder and String Quartet, though formally it was rather stricter than its predecessor with this title, the solo Recorder Fantasy. Arnold ingeniously cast the new work as theme and variations in five linked movements and bound it together by making the opening of the piece contain the germ of all that follows. The short sequence of movements was carefully varied in rhythm and tempo, while the soloist's recorder skills were fully stretched: she was required to use three different members of the recorder family – sopranino, descant and treble – and also to sing into the instrument while playing, a skill she had demonstrated to him the first time they met.

The Recorder Fantasy was the best of the four works to emerge from this year. It was gratifying that people still wanted him to write music for them and there were commissions on the stocks. Ross Pople, who with his London Festival Orchestra had made an acclaimed recording of some of the Sinfoniettas and Concertos, wanted a Sinfonia Concertante from the composer for a planned seventieth birthday concert in the Queen Elizabeth Hall. The Incorporated Association of Preparatory Schools Orchestra, of which Arnold was President, asked for an orchestral work for a London concert in 1992. Arnold, responsive to the needs of young performers, accepted and even offered a title: *A Flavour of Ischia*. He and Anthony Day had been to stay at Walton's old home on this Mediterranean island at Lady Walton's request and the new piece would repay something of his debt to his old friend. Even so, judged only by the yardstick of Arnold's own music from earlier years, it was clear to others, if not to the composer himself, that he was doing himself and his reputation no good with his most recent work. It was left to Anthony Day, on the doctors' advice, finally to discourage him from continuing to write. The Sinfonia Concertante and *A Flavour of Ischia* remained unwritten.

The composer himself had recognised at the time of the Ninth Symphony, four years earlier, that the effort of a further symphony was likely to be beyond him. His publishers, too, had grown increasingly concerned. Times for music publishers were more difficult than ever in a fierce recession when music simply did not sell in adequate quantities. Faber Music printed the first of the Michala Petri pieces, the Cello Fantasy and a brief new Brass Quintet for the Fine Arts Brass Ensemble and accepted the Recorder Concerto, but then called a halt. The Paterson and Lengnick catalogues were both sold to other owners, the uncertainties over these sales causing Arnold much anxiety. Paterson's was first acquired by Peters Edition and then by Novello, who also took on Arnold's final handful of works, before reluctantly deciding that no more would be printed. The news, when Anthony Day broke it to him, was painful – but perhaps not a surprise. In effect, Malcolm Arnold retired from composition at the end of 1991.

These late years also increasingly brought to mind a parallel that had surfaced in Arnold's student years, when he had first encountered the maverick figure of Constant Lambert. Because of Lambert's early death, in 1951, the two had not known each other well for any length of time. Yet subconsciously, the older man became almost something of a role model for the younger. There is the same chapter of domestic accidents: Lambert's marriages both failed – his second wife was even called Isabel[4] – he took refuge from the world in the pubs of London and became virtually alcoholic, he had a strong rebellious, debunking streak, combined with a sharp wit and a love of the good things of life. As Andrew Motion records in his study of the Lambert clan, the pressures on Constant towards the end of his life were immense, resembling those on Arnold at the height of his activity in films; and these pressures, combined with drink and undiagnosed diabetes, eventually killed him.

Ironically, Arnold's withdrawal from creative work coincided with his seventieth birthday year and a sudden spate of interest in the composer and his music. Compact discs appeared in increasing number, covering a substantial portion of his output. He was still prepared to accept occasional conducting engagements, mostly for recordings. He continued to travel, either accepting invitations from foreign orchestras, or on holidays to the sun. He was interviewed regularly and was mostly ready to co-operate. Guest appearances at concerts and musical functions began to fill his diary. Even the reviews began at last to become warmer, and the *Gramophone* in particular seemed to greet each new release with enthusiasm. Birthday milestones often resulted in public celebrations: both his sixty-fifth and seventieth birthdays were celebrated on the South Bank in London and the latter almost turned into an on-stage party, complete with cake and seventy candles – which he had no difficulty extinguishing with a single trumpeter's lungful.

And Arnold certainly enjoyed the honours that increasingly came his way, accepting them as no less than his due. He saw them as marks of long-overdue public approbation and encouragement, as well as of academic respectability: honorary doctorates from Exeter, Durham, Miami University in Ohio, Leicester and Trinity College London, the recognition by the Bards of the Cornish Gorsedd, the conferring of a Fellowship of the Royal College of Music in 1983 and his appearances in the Honours List. Recognition by his own profession was important too: to his earlier Ivor Novello award in the Fifties was added a similar award in 1989 and this time it was for 'outstanding services to music', a tribute which touched him deeply. The climax, in the 1993 New Year Honours, was his knighthood, engineered by vigorous lobbying of the sympathetic Arts Minister, David Mellor, by Arnold's old friend and briefly his agent, Archie Newman.

In concerts and broadcasts, less familiar corners of the Arnold repertoire began to be explored as well. In 1991, for the biennial Comic Relief fund-raising day which had come to be known universally as Red Nose Day because the organisers had devised the brilliantly simple notion of issuing a plastic red nose to all contributors, the BBC alighted on a piece of Malcolm Arnold's, long buried in obscurity, as a suitable contribution to the occasion. A listener pledged a generous sum to Comic Relief for a performance of the Greyfriars School Song, Billy Bunter's old school – a long out-of-print *Greyfriars Annual* had once contained a setting by Arnold of Frank Richards's words. A copy was obtained from the British Library and the song duly performed by a group of Radio 3 announcers wearing sporting kit and the appropriate red noses. After the broadcast, copies of the resulting photograph were also auctioned off and several hundred pounds duly raised for Comic Relief. The clowning instinct in Malcolm Arnold was still infectious.

Maybe it had its roots in his brass-playing youth – once a trumpeter, always a trumpeter. Though he had scarcely touched the trumpet since leaving the LPO and seldom taught the instrument, he remained a keen observer of the brass scene, taking pride for instance in the emergence, in the Seventies and Eighties, of a fine new generation of British trumpeters: Philip Jones, Elgar Howarth, Howard Snell, John Wilbraham and John Wallace among them. Many of them, like Arnold, kept a foot in the brass-band camp as well, conducting his Little Suites and particularly the Fantasy for Brass Band, and occasionally consulting the composer on matters of interpretation. The Fantasy quickly became a staple diet of the band repertoire after fulfilling its initial function of test piece for the Brass Band Championships of 1969, at which it was performed no fewer than nineteen times in succession. In the brass-band world, Malcolm Arnold still seemed to be in his element.

So, while his health in these latter years continued to fluctuate, sometimes to Anthony Day's alarm, Arnold continued to do almost everything except compose. Reconciliations were even effected. Isobel Arnold – in the last few years of her life – visited him in Norfolk and London, attended the seventieth birthday events and a recording session conducted by Richard Hickox of some of the film music and, from 1987, allowed her ex-husband access to their autistic son Edward in his sheltered accommodation in Kent. The culmination of the 1991 seventieth birthday celebrations, though, took place in the month after the event. The composer's agent, Georgina Ivor, had devoted much time and energy in the months, even years, before his birthday to interesting performers and promoters in the idea of using the occasion to resurrect old scores, promising personal appearances by the composer and, hopefully, some attendant publicity at the time. She had reckoned without the continuing nervousness of the musical establishment about the ability of any twentieth-century composer, let alone a home-grown one apart from Sir Michael Tippett or Benjamin Britten, to break even at the box office. Undaunted, she tried another tack: a concentration of events in a particular place, involving all the musical organisations available, professional or amateur, symphony or chamber, and particularly those with regular series and audiences and, therefore, with tried and trusted venues. Slowly the idea of an Arnold birthday festival was formed[5] – and eventually realised.

The first of the many problems was where to hold it. This was quickly solved. Manchester seemed a heaven-sent location. In the past Arnold had had connections with the Hallé Orchestra – he had for instance conducted the world première of the Fifth Symphony with them in Cheltenham. Sir Edward Downes, then in the final year of his long tenure of office as Principal Conductor of the BBC Philharmonic, had a known interest in the Arnold symphonies and a willingness to programme unfamiliar repertoire. The management of the BBC Philharmonic, Trevor Green, Peter Marchbank and later Brian Pidgeon, were all Arnold enthusiasts. With dates promised from these two prominent Mancunian institutions Georgina Ivor could go ahead and canvass others in the city.

By a monumental effort of persuasion, a great many other local musical bodies were persuaded to come on board and the month of November 1991 provided Manchester, and Malcolm Arnold, with a concentrated feast of his music such as a living British composer had seldom experienced. The educational establishments, in the form of Manchester University, the Royal Northern College of Music, Salford College of Technology and Cheetham's School of Music, were particularly supportive, while groups such as the Manchester Camerata and the Northern Chamber Orchestra, run by Arnold's old friend the composer David Ellis who had helped with the concert version of the ballet *Sweeney Todd*, were persuaded to include a work in their winter tours, with the further result that the festival spread to other towns such as Sheffield, Kendal, Lancaster, Bolton and Macclesfield.

One other early key resolution was a decisive element in its success and altered its character substantially. Because Manchester had played host, three years previously, to a festival combining the music of Tippett with Debussy, and also as a concession to market forces, Georgina Ivor decided to repeat the idea. Again the choice of the twin composer was easy, and the event became known as the Arnold–Haydn Celebration. There was much in common between the two composers: musical wit and humour above all, but also a profound belief in the symphony as a form of musical expression and even a shared trust in Enlightenment values about human dignity and social ideals. Arnold himself was delighted with the coupling: 'I feel I have more affinity with Haydn than with any other composer . . . I used to love playing Haydn when I was a trumpeter; not many others did.'[6]

When, attending the Manchester concerts during the Celebration, he found himself listening to the infinite variety not just of many quartets and symphonies, but of Haydn Masses, part-songs, the Trumpet Concerto and even a brass-band arrangement of one of the *Seven Last Words*, his mind inevitably went back to those youthful attempts with Jim Aspinall at four-hand piano arrangements of Haydn, when records came only in the shape of expensive 78s, the Third Programme did not exist, but still the genius of the wizard of Eisenstadt shone through. Such memories seemed a lifetime ago.

Surprisingly, one work was missing from the orchestral programmes in the Festival. No one chose to pick up the connection between Arnold's *Peterloo* Overture and the city, yet the drama it portrays had taken place on St Peter's Fields in Manchester in 1819. The Overture would have been appropriate for inclusion in the Arnold–Haydn Celebration for other reasons as well. The Festival's eventual success was achieved against considerable odds, notably a lack of any central funding or sponsorship. All the concerts were put on by the bodies concerned. There was simply no money available to fund any kind of central Festival umbrella, apart from a limited contribution from Arnold's three publishers for a leaflet. At least one concert nearly came to grief in a bitter dispute over hire fees and whether they could be afforded.

One event that stood out in this month of intensive music-making came when Sir Charles Groves directed the Britten Singers and the BBC Philharmonic in Haydn's *Mass in Time of War* and boldly coupled it with Arnold's Seventh Symphony. The Arnold performance was intense and deeply felt, Groves taking a different view of the piece from previous interpreters such as Edward Downes or Vernon Handley. The violence in the score was still present, but less hectically pursued than at other times, while its moments of relaxation loomed larger than before and the symphony seemed more balanced, less nihilistic, in consequence. After the concert, with the composer and BBC representatives both present, Groves was invited to return and to set right an injustice that had long troubled him, the veil of silence that had overtaken another Arnold symphony since its eventual completion: the Ninth.

As if intended by fate, there was an unexpected space in the diaries of both conductor and orchestra early the following year. As a result, on Monday 20 January 1992 in Studio 7 at BBC Manchester, the BBC Philharmonic gave the world première. The composer himself was once again present for the occasion, officially an invitation concert for the friends of the BBC Philharmonic, recorded for a later broadcast. The new Symphony was the sole piece in the concert.

Groves had already conducted a run-through of the work for the composer's benefit early in 1988 in Greenwich, with the Orchestra of the National Centre for Orchestral Studies (now disbanded). Groves believed in the piece and at his insistence efforts to secure a first professional and public performance elsewhere continued. They came to nothing; although the Bournemouth Symphony Orchestra, who had long ago given the première of the Second Symphony with Groves, originally scheduled it as part of an Arnold seventieth birthday celebration of their own, they then withdrew, fearing audience incomprehension.

It was not until the showing of a film by Kriss Rusmanis about Malcolm Arnold in BBC 1's 'Omnibus' series, timed to coincide with his seventieth birthday, that the tide began to turn. The film included specially filmed shots of Arnold conducting the closing pages of the Ninth Symphony and an implicit plea for natural justice to be done. Which it was, on a foggy night in Manchester just a couple of months later.

Ever since Beethoven, writing a Ninth Symphony has been for a composer something akin to climbing Mount Everest – the summit, the summation even, of a lifetime's achievement. In addition, there has come to be something fatalistic about the very idea of a Ninth Symphony. To take two examples from the twentieth century, Bruckner died before he could complete what would have been the longest of his symphonies, while Mahler's Ninth was written in the shadow of his fatal illness. Shostakovich – much admired by Malcolm Arnold, who claimed[7] that his Russian contemporary spoke English much better than he pretended and that they had had several illuminating conversations – was so over-awed by the burden of this musical tradition that he deliberately stood it on its head and wrote a lightweight piece. Arnold himself admitted to being daunted by the weight of musical history; not surprisingly, since his Ninth was conceived after a period during which his life had reached the lowest ebb it was possible to imagine.[8]

Malcolm Arnold's Ninth Symphony has four movements – but that innocent restatement of a familiar enough pattern does not reveal the surprises in store. First comes a triple-time allegro, a departure from previous models in that it is not really dramatic as in earlier Arnold symphonic openings. If anything it is rather naïve in character, the themes being not so much developed as given a wide variety of different orchestral colourings. The only real climax is saved for the end of the movement, where the tempo slows while pitch and dynamics increase almost to breaking-point. One of the most disturbing features of the Ninth for performers and critics alike is the amount of straightforward – or sometimes not so straightforward – repetition, a procedure familiar enough from classical models but unexpected in the late twentieth century. There is also much unison instrumental writing, adding to the impression of economy. The second movement is memorable: a gentle, pastoral allegretto in nine-eight time, with much of the writing in just two or three parts and based on a haunting, melancholy modal tune that resembles a folk-like carol. The echoes of Holst or Vaughan Williams in Malcolm Arnold's early music seem to surface again in old age. The third movement is a noisy two-four piece marked giubiloso and not unlike many another breezy Arnold scherzo, with much prominent and solo tricky writing for the wind, particularly the brass, and full of characteristic Arnold clashes and dissonances within a tonal framework.

It is with the finale that the balance of the Ninth Symphony changes and the whole work takes on a new aspect. It lasts almost as long as the other three movements put together and it is not the usual quick symphonic finale but a huge slow movement – just like the anguished adagio finales of Tchaikovsky's *Pathétique* Symphony, or of another Ninth, that of Gustav Mahler. Arnold himself confirmed the parallels.[9] However, the emotional feel is different from Mahler, and is peculiar to Arnold alone: there is for instance none of Mahler's frenzy. Almost throughout, the movement is bleak and intense, spare and grief-stricken; like a gigantic funeral march, it forsakes dramatic contrasts for the sake of an unbroken continuity of atmosphere, until the final bars which form a radiant resolution on to D major. Without this chord, the surrender to nihilism and despair would be total. 'D major sings to eternity.'[10]

In purely musical terms the material of this finale is often very simple, haunted throughout by the falling phrase of the opening; but at the same time it is extremely demanding, both on the players in terms of concentration and on the listener in terms of its emotional journey. A couplet from the Welsh poet Dylan Thomas, nowhere quoted or mentioned by the composer, nevertheless seems not too distant from the Ninth Symphony's spirit and temper:

> Do not go gentle into that good night.
> Rage, rage against the dying of the light.

Finale

The Universal Frame

Malcolm Arnold's Ninth Symphony had a potent if uncomfortable message. Conducting the première, Sir Charles Groves knew this, and it informed his reading with authority and dignity. He also knew he could do the symphony differently, maybe even better, under different circumstances. Tragically, his heart attack a few short months later precluded this possibility. His appearance in Manchester that January, conducting the music of a man he had long admired and championed, turned out to be one of the last occasions on which he conducted.

Sir Charles Groves's death upset Malcolm Arnold greatly, offering a grim reminder of mortality, and even of the capriciousness of death. He knew what he owed to his friend and on one occasion[1] declared that Sir Charles's recording of the English Dances was better than his own. Arnold's second wife, Isobel, also died in the course of the year. His wider family remained at a distance. The past could not easily be undone. The present was to be born as stoically as possible. The future was not to be thought about at all.

Asking a composer how he wants to be remembered is not always the kindest of questions. Arnold, though, had an answer ready for Michael Oliver:[2] all he wanted, he said, was for posterity to think of him, if it did at all, as 'an honest composer'. On another occasion[3] he quoted *The Tempest*, Prospero's line about

> Sounds, and sweet airs, that give delight,
> and hurt not,

and hoped that he had achieved something similar.

The achievement, though, is considerably greater than Arnold's own estimation allows. For a start, Arnold's voice over the whole range of his music from the 1940s to the 1990s, from the nine symphonies to the film scores, is recognisably individual. It was recognised as such by the audiences who went to concerts of his music, or heard it in the cinema, or bought it on gramophone records. If the critics chose to be condescending Arnold, though wounded, had an answer. Challenged to say if he felt unjustly neglected, Arnold pointed[4] to the honours he had accumulated and to the genuine affection he experienced from performers and listeners alike.

Nor was he always quite so lonely a figure. Plenty of figures in the English Musical Renaissance could be so seen and were often described as isolationist. It is no coincidence that in discussing Arnold, the names of Berlioz, Mahler, Sibelius and even Schoenberg occur far more frequently than those of, say, Parry or Stanford, Bax or Ireland, even Vaughan Williams or Holst. The English folk-song revival, with which they were associated and whose pastoral idiom frequently found its way into English music of their generation, passed him by – more completely so even than it did Benjamin Britten, for whom folk-song had a definite place in his unconscious and sometimes conscious creative drive.

Reading about the lives of other English composers, Britten or Tippett for instance, one cannot help being struck that they have often been surrounded by a coterie of admirers who have functioned as sounding-boards for ideas, projects and ambitions, who have provided admiring first audiences, and also acted as buffer zones between the composer and critics of all kinds, whether in the media or from the public. Conspicuously, Arnold lacked such keen protection in earlier years, and only acquired it, in the shape of Anthony Day, when it became an almost medical necessity. For the most part, he was on his own. And this confidence in his own chosen path makes Malcolm Arnold less recognisably English a composer than some of his contemporaries. This has a great deal to do with his attitude to words and music. The art of composers such as Holst and Vaughan Williams, Britten and Tippett, is vocal in its roots, even when they are writing instrumental music. Like only a handful of other British composers this century – Havergal Brian, Robert Simpson, Edmund Rubbra – Arnold was first and foremost an orchestral thinker, a symphonist not dependent on words or on extra-musical ideas. The dearth of vocal music in Arnold's output certainly does not imply a lack of sensitivity to words: speaking of his own settings of Blake for contralto and string orchestra he described William Blake as 'a God of mine' and declared that he revered him for his mysticism, his paintings and his poetry. Yet Arnold deliberately denied himself the riches of English literature as a potential quarry. The dramatic gifts and instincts which David Lean so shrewdly observed in him were channelled not towards the stage, but towards a medium which – though he eventually forced himself to abandon it – he adorned as few other composers have done or will do. The cinema claimed him for its own. If it had not, and the operatic stage had exercised a more powerful allure, his musical language would certainly not have been found wanting, neither would the English operatic repertoire have been so harshly denied a major Arnold contribution.

Film liberated Malcolm Arnold at the same time that it made him its prisoner. He was surely right to regard the two sides of his activity as indivisible. Asked whether his style changed when writing symphonies as opposed to film scores, his reply was unequivocal: 'I've always said that any music I write, whether film, concert hall, ballet or chamber music, I just write what I would like to hear. John Addison once said to me, "You're very lucky, Malcolm, you don't have to think about what style you write in." I said, "Good God, if you think about that, you'll never get started. You've just got to write and make it your own."'[5]

And this sureness in his own voice enabled him to quarry at will in other sources and styles when the occasion demanded. The language of popular music, when it occurs in the Fourth and Fifth Symphonies for example, is not a concession to current fashion but an integral part of the musical argument. It can thus be made to sit alongside passages based on the twelve-tone methods of Schoenberg, or symphonically-adapted *marches militaires*, or sardonic imitations of the music-hall or the circus. Humour and deep seriousness sit side by side, in art as in life – the epigraph to this book, from Angela Carter's *Nights at the Circus*, says as much in its wonderful description of the clown, old Buffo, declaiming his credo. Malcolm Arnold was the least theoretical of composers but, paradoxically, he was at the same time a man of very strong beliefs, which the whole of his music expresses.

Any verdict on Malcolm Arnold must necessarily be provisional. But it is possible to form some notion of the place in musical history to which he can lay claim. His skill as a melodist of the first order emphasises his links with the nineteenth century, with Berlioz and with Mahler, and he shares their propensity to shock tactics: for all three, truth is sometimes as important as beauty – though not more so, which is the accusation he made against some of his contemporaries.[6] In this sense, and in the sense of his admired William Blake, Malcolm Arnold is a man of both Innocence and Experience. In him, the two collide occasionally, but harmonise often. He is for the light against the dark, though the dark often threatens to win the fight. He is for the translucent against the hermetic, though much remains hidden in his music. He is for the enduring substance of tradition against the vagaries of fashion, though this does not prevent him from being an unashamed eclectic. Arnold is also for pure music against the naïvely programmatic, though he has written programme music, and for commitment via musical argument as opposed to the strident clamour of rhetoric and slogan – yet his music speaks in broad brush-strokes and uses the language of the people.

Out of this maze of paradox, he emerges as on the whole an

optimist who remained so throughout his composing life. The D major chord at the end of the Ninth Symphony's adagio was an affirmation of this belief. If this consistency has sometimes been criticised as a lack of development, the charge does not stand up. Those who make it confuse fertility with facility and do not see that the universal spirit also requires an individual voice for its expression. Malcolm Arnold, seeing – as a universal spirit must – that his art encompasses, but also goes far beyond, the pleasure principle, has in over half a century of music-making truly found his own individual voice. It is to his credit, and our enrichment, that it is audible in every bar of his mature music.

Two Articles on Music by Malcolm Arnold

I. *I think of music in terms of sound*

I write music because it is only possible to express the ideas and emotions I wish to express through the medium of music.

Music appeals to me chiefly because of its abstract quality. It is not necessarily tied to a story or a subject. That is the reason why most of my works are orchestral or chamber music, and although I have written a certain amount of vocal music, for me the most worthwhile thoughts are to be expressed without words.

I do not have any theory about the ways of putting notes together, but I have a number of strong beliefs which are the basis of all my work, and possibly some day, if anyone listens without prejudice to all my music, he will be able to see clearly what these beliefs are, and, no doubt, decide whether they have been worthwhile.

When a composer writes a phrase for a performer he should be acutely aware that the person he is asking to play his phrase is someone to whom the performing of music is just as important as the composing of music is to the composer. Therefore this is a responsible task and not to be approached lightly. One must know that the phrase is absolutely necessary to the whole work and that it is written in such a way as to give the player the finest possible chance to show himself at his best.

In the eight years I spent as an orchestral player I spent many hours practising difficult passages from all kinds of works, contemporary and otherwise, knowing full well that the result of them in performance would be to clutter up an already over-thick texture.

This sort of thing, of course, does not encourage a player to give of his best, and when one arrives at a place in the composition when one's instrument (in the immortal phrase of Sir Henry Wood) must 'tell', one is too exhausted for this to be possible. The number of climaxes in music that have suffered because of these circumstances is too numerous to mention!

Another point which is always in my mind is that of development. If one is *really* honest in listening to the music of all periods there are times when one's mind is inclined to wander. This will happen even when listening to accepted classical masterpieces, and to a greater extent when listening to contemporary works. To put it crudely, the mind wanders during the sections that occur in music between the recognisable themes – always assuming that the theme or themes have said something to the listener.

Very, very roughly speaking, these parts of a composition are usually development sections; one cannot write a piece of music by just repeating one theme, unless it is a special effect one is after as in Ravel's *Bolero*. A composer has to compose something that contrasts and will show his original thought in a new light, and the play between these two or three or even more thoughts goes to make up a composition.

To hold a listener's attention throughout a whole work is a major problem.

Composers during the whole short history of written music have used all kinds of devices to develop their music and give it formal continuity. One can use the first few notes of the original thought by themselves, one can use the original thought backwards, or as a rhythmic pattern, making a new melody out of it; one can use its harmonic pattern and a new idea may spring from that.

The ways of continuing or developing music are legion, but an important point which we composers in our enthusiasm as specialists in music are apt to forget is that these ways in themselves are of no interest to anyone. The music must say more to the listener than 'I am the first three notes of the original thought' or 'I am the original thought backwards'. What this something more is, is impossible to define in words; which will help to explain why I search after this elusive something only by writing music.

To use two of my favourite composers as examples: one can find in some late Sibelius works perfect unity and form in performance, and yet to the eye there is no apparent connection at all between the musical statements. In some works of Mahler one can find every kind of technical connection between statements by looking at the score, and yet in performance the unity and form of the music is often difficult to grasp. This slight obstacle which I have to surmount to enjoy some of Mahler's original and beautiful music is so small as not to detract from it as a whole.

Since Mahler's death very few composers have used the wonderfully clear and clean sounds which he used to such perfection, and I can see endless possibilities, stretching into the distant future, of creating new music within the limits of the tonal system if one always thinks in terms of sound and not only of notes on paper.

The greatest musical influence in my life has been, and still is, the music of Berlioz. His compositions always strike me as so fresh, and far more contemporary in spirit than so much of the music written only a few days ago. If he can express his idea by a melody only he does so, and if it is a melody based on tonic and dominant harmonies (which would have been considered by some as 'old fashioned' in his day) he is not afraid to do so. At times within a tonic and dominant context he will astonish by a harmonic change which is decidedly 'not done' – which goes to prove once again that so many of the things which are so well worth doing are decidedly 'not done'.

Sometimes, when I am annoyed by reading a critic dismiss all of my work on the basis of one appalling performance he has just heard, I think of all the stupid arguments that are still brought forward when the name of such a giant as Berlioz is mentioned, and I thank my lucky stars that I am in the fortunate position of being able to earn a living by writing music and not by writing about music.

When I am asked to write music for a ballet, a school orchestra, a film or a revue, I write exactly what I would like to hear if I were to go to the particular entertainment for which the music has been commissioned. On quite a number of occasions my ideas have coincided with other people's – from which you will gather that my stars have been lucky indeed!

First published in *Music and Musicians*,
July 1956

II. *Don't shoot the pianist*

There is no possible justification for the arrogant, high-minded way in which British music critics treat musicians. These critics are a standing joke throughout the world, and there are a number of great artists who will not perform in Britain because of the offensiveness of British critics. It is sad to think that this is one of the few positive effects they have had on the music of this country. There is such a general lack of understanding of the nature of music and the nature of performing music that the dogmas arising from ignorance of the subject lead to a narrow conformity.

Our music critics, with two notable exceptions, are people who are unable to perform or compose, and have not enough musical knowledge to be able to give elementary music lessons. When one is aware of this, it is absolutely astounding to read the rude and arrogant way in which they write about musicians of far greater ability than their own. Even if a person had the necessary musical knowledge, attendance at a concert or recital every day and sometimes twice a day throughout the year would kill any balanced approach to the art, and I would suggest that the money wasted in paying music critics should be used in the following way: a practising musician should be engaged for only one week at a time to report musical performances, and there should be a panel of at least a hundred people to do this work. They would then approach music with the attitude that it is an act of friendship and something to enjoy, and not something merely to talk about.

The majority of criticisms of performers or composers, I have noticed, bear little relationship to what has happened at a concert. In fact it would be possible to write accurately the criticisms that will appear, before the concert takes place. By this I mean that certain artists who are either 'in' or 'out' will always get the same criticisms, regardless of what they do. This is another instance of the narrowness of outlook that is caused by ignorance of the subject.

The only music which we are allowed to call modern by our critics is music that has a distinct flavour and sound which, to an educated musician, spells the twenties. This makes concert promoters nervous of putting on any modern music which is not the 'in' type of modern music, which means that a great deal of interesting and well worthwhile music composed in this country is never heard publicly and never will be, while the narrow conformity of outlook on modern music continues to hold sway.

I should be sorry in some ways to see any alteration in our music criticism, because the astounding gaffes that are made every day are a source of constant amusement to all musicians. A typical example of this sort of thing which happened recently was a criticism of the Britten Serenade for Tenor, Horn, and Strings, when the brilliant, virtuoso horn player was severely taken to task by the critic because he was out of tune in the prelude and postlude where, as everybody knows, the composer asks that this should be played on the natural harmonics of the instrument, which are, in fact, to our ears, slightly out of tune. Examples of this type are too numerous to mention, and in a strange way are so funny that they do add some joy to this otherwise dismal occupation. Throughout history the day-to-day writing about music has always been wrong, and I would have thought that in the knowledge of this historical fact anybody writing today would be more careful and have more respect for the people they are writing about.

Let us say down, down, down with the music critics before they make our music the arid and joyless music of the concentration camp.

First published in the *Guardian*,
3 June 1971

Notes

Unless otherwise indicated, references are to the sources indicated in the Select Bibliography. Much of Malcolm Arnold's story has been told to the author in the course of many conversations or broadcasts, the *Contrasts* interview regularly referred to below was a series of intensive sessions filmed for a TV portrait.

Chapter One

1. William Arnold, p. 8
2. Rubbra, p. 7
3. MA to Christopher Ford
4. MA to Murray Schafer, p. 151
5. MA to PBP, *Contrasts*
6. ibid.
7. ibid.
8. MA, 'My Early Life', p. 8
9. Blades, *Drum Roll*, pp. 93–4
10. MA, 'My Early Life', p. 8
11. MA to PBP, *Contrasts*
12. Adeney, p. 24
13. Adeney, ibid.
14. Adeney, ibid.
15. Russell, passim
16. MA, 'My Early Life', p. 9
17. Motion, p. 133
18. Margaret Archibald, sleeve note to record HMV ASD 3823
19. MA to Christopher Ford

Chapter Two

1. MA to Christopher Ford
2. MA, 'My Early Life', p. 9
3. MA to PBP, *Contrasts. Beckus the Dandipratt* was issued as a 78 on Decca K 1844. The cornet was played by his friend and LPO colleague Denis Egan.
4. Temple Savage, p. 93

5. Ibid., p. 100
6. Bernstein to Copland, letter of 9 June 1946, quoted in Burton, p. 149
7. Pettitt, p. 101
8. The others were by Edward Michael and Jeffrey Mark
9. Railton, p. 45
10. ibid., p. 46
11. ibid., p. 46
12. ibid., p. 67
13. ibid., p. 171
14. More than forty years later, Thurston's widow the clarinettist Thea King made an excellent recording of both of MA's clarinet concertos
15. see Chapter Three, passim
16. Cole, *Introduction*, p. 40
17. ibid., p. 228
18. Margaret Archibald, sleeve note to record HMV ASD 3823

Chapter Three

Epigraph: MA to Christopher Ritchie

1. MA to Murray Schafer, p. 150
2. Amis, p. 193
3. MA to Kenneth Eastaugh, *Daily Sketch*, 24 September 1969
4. Mitchell, 'Malcolm Arnold', pp. 410–3
5. MA to Murray Schafer, p. 151
6. As he was later to do for Greyfriars, Billy Bunter's old school!
7. MA, 'Writing for Films', talk for BBC Transcription Service, 25 July 1961
8. MA to Murray Schafer, p. 150
9. Peacock, 'Arnold at 60'
10. see 'Films' for full listing
11. MA to Christopher Ritchie
12. David Lean, letter to MA, 4 February 1958

Chapter Four

Epigraph: MA, *Music and Musicians*, July 1956, p. 9

1. Transcript of *Desert Island Discs*, BBC Home Service, 1959
2. MA to *Dundee Courier*, 28 May 1987
3. MA to Christopher Ford
4. MA to PBP, *Contrasts*
5. Brymer, p. 188

6. MA, programme note for first performance
7. Adeney, p. 86
8. In the programme book for MA's sixty-fifth birthday concert, Queen Elizabeth Hall, 21 October 1986
9. Palmer, p. 81
10. ibid.
11. Paul Hamburger, letter to PBP, 12 October 1982
12. Adler, p. 211
13. Pettitt, p. 148
14. Amis, pp. 114–5
15. ibid., p. 193
16. Lionel Salter, letter to PBP, 30 November 1986
17. MA to PBP
18. Vaughan, p. 433
19. MA to PBP, interview for broadcast of *Homage to the Queen*, BBC Radio 3, November 1993
20. MA to Christopher Ritchie
21. ibid.

Chapter Five

Epigraph: MA to PBP, *Contrasts*

1. and in oblique homage to William Walton as well
2. MA to PBP, *Contrasts*
3. MA, programme note for first performance
4. MA to Christopher Ford
5. ibid.
6. Yet Bruckner was never one of MA's stronger enthusiasms
7. MA, note in published score
8. Peter Gammond, sleeve note to record Decca SB 313
9. MA to PBP, *Contrasts*. Arnold's carol appeared in the *Daily Telegraph* magazine on 22 December 1967
10. ibid.
11. Fritz Spiegl, letter to PBP
12. MA to PBP, *Contrasts*
13. MA to Christopher Ritchie
14. ibid. The main tune in *The Reckoning* is based on the Irish folk melody 'The Harp that once in Tara's halls'
15. ibid.
16. ibid.
17. MA, letter to Stewart Craggs, quoted in Poulton, *Catalogue*, p. 171
18. MA to PBP, *Contrasts*
19. MA, in the *Listener*, 14 October 1971, p. 518

Chapter Six

Epigraph: MA to Margaret Howard

1. MA to PBP, *Contrasts*
2. MA to Christopher Ford
3. MA, in the *Listener*, 14 October 1971, p. 518
4. MA, programme note for first performance
5. see Mitchell, 'Malcolm Arnold'
6. MA, preface to published score, Faber Music
7. Harries, p. 197
8. Simpson, passim
9. MA, programme note for first performance
10. MA to David Munrow
11. MA in *The Times*, 14 May 1959
12. Keller, 'The crisis of the string quartet', the *Listener*, 13 April 1974, p. 494
13. anonymous review, *Sunday Times*, 11 October 1992
14. MA to Paul Fisher, *Sunday Telegraph*, 6 October 1991
15. MA, programme note for first performance
16. MA to PBP, *Contrasts*
17. The Foundation had made a feature of commissioning British composers; others included Edmund Rubbra and George Lloyd
18. MA to Margaret Howard, Classic FM, 21 October 1992
19. Amis, p. 193
20. MA to PBP, *Contrasts*

Chapter Seven

Epigraph: MA to Christopher Ford

1. Adeney, p. 87
2. MA to PBP, *Contrasts*
3. McDonald, p. 87
4. MA to PBP, *Contrasts*
5. the author
6. Keller, *Criticism*, p. 31. In the same book Keller documents the psychological damage he believes was inflicted on Benjamin Britten by critical hostility and misunderstanding
7. MA to John Amis, BBC World Service, 17 October 1986

Chapter Eight

Epigraph: Anthony Day to PBP

1. MA to PBP, *Contrasts*
2. MA to *Dundee Courier*, 28 May 1987

3. MA, programme note for first performance
4. Isabel Lambert was previously married to the foreign correspondent Sefton Delmer. After Lambert's death she married the composer Alan Rawsthorne
5. The author must declare an interest as musical adviser to the Arnold–Haydn Celebration
6. MA to Peter Paul Nash
7. ibid.
8. ibid.
9. ibid. In the same interview, MA disclaimed any affinity with another composer of a fateful Ninth, Bruckner
10. ibid.

Finale

1. MA to PBP, *Contrasts*
2. MA to Michael Oliver, BBC Radio 3, 20 January 1980
3. MA to PBP, *Contrasts*
4. MA to John Amis, BBC World Service, 17 October 1986
5. MA to Christopher Ritchie
6. MA to Murray Schafer, p. 154

List of Works

The following work list gives brief details of title, date of composition (if available, otherwise first performance when known, occasionally publication) and publisher. For fuller information, the principal source up to 1986 is Alan Poulton's *The Music of Malcolm Arnold: A Catalogue*, published by Faber and Faber. This contains details of duration, first performance, instrumentation and publication. It also lists the music both chronologically and by category and documents all the composer's film scores, incidental music for radio and television, arrangements and juvenilia, and includes an exhaustive discography. It is usefully supplemented by the publishers' catalogues periodically issued by Alfred Lengnick & Co., Faber Music and Novello & Co. who now own the former Paterson catalogue.

Works with opus number

1 Divertimento for orchestra, f.p. 1945. Lost
2 Wind Quintet, f.p. 1943. Lost
3 Tone Poem, *Larch Trees*, 1943. Faber
4 *Three Shanties* for wind quintet, f.p. 1943. Paterson
5 Overture, *Beckus the Dandipratt*, 1943. Lengnick
6 Trio for flute, viola and bassoon, 1943. Paterson
7 Quintet for flute, violin, viola, horn and bassoon, f.p. 1944. Paterson
8 Two songs for voice and piano, f.p. 1947. Novello
9 *Variations on a Ukrainian Folk Song*, for solo piano, f.p. 1946. Lengnick
10 Duo for flute and viola, 1945. Faber
11 Concerto no. 1 for horn and orchestra, 1945. Lengnick
12 Symphonic Suite for orchestra. Lost

13 Symphony for strings, f.p. 1947. Lengnick
14 *Festival Overture*, f.p. 1946. Lengnick
15 Sonata no. 1 for violin and piano, 1947. Lengnick
16 *Children's Suite* for piano, pub. 1948. Lengnick
17 Sonata for viola and piano, 1947. Lengnick
18 Two Bagatelles for solo piano, 1947. Paterson
19 Sonatina for flute and piano, 1948. Lengnick
20 Concerto for clarinet and strings, 1948. Lengnick
21 Overture, *The Smoke*, 1948. Lengnick
22 Symphony no. 1, 1949. Lengnick
23 String Quartet no. 1, 1949. Lengnick
24 Divertimento no. 2 for orchestra, 1950. Paterson. (Revised and published as opus 75)
25 Psalm 150 (*Laudate Dominum*), for chorus and organ, 1950. Lengnick
26 Serenade for small orchestra, 1950. Lengnick
27 English Dances (Set 1), 1950. Lengnick
28 Sonatina for oboe and piano, 1951. Lengnick
29 Sonatina for clarinet and piano, 1951. Lengnick
30 Symphonic Study, *Machines*, 1951. Faber
31 *A Sussex Overture*, 1951. Lengnick
32 Concerto for piano duet and strings, 1951. Lengnick
33 English Dances (Set 2), 1951. Lengnick
34 Opera in one act, *The Dancing Master*, 1952. Novello
35 Two Ceremonial Psalms, f.p. 1952. Paterson
36 Eight Children's Pieces for solo piano, pub. 1952. Lengnick
37 Divertimento for wind trio, f.p. 1953. Paterson
38 Rhapsody, *The Sound Barrier*, 1952. Paterson
39 Concerto for oboe and strings, 1952. Paterson
40 Second Symphony, 1953. Paterson
41 Sonatina for recorder and piano, 1953. Paterson
42 Ballet, *Homage to the Queen*, 1953. Paterson
43 Sonata no. 2 for violin and piano, f.p. 1953. Paterson
44 *Flourish for a 21st birthday*, f.p. 1953. Studio Music
45 Concerto no. 1 for flute and strings, 1954. Paterson
46 Concerto for harmonica and orchestra, 1954. Paterson
47 Concerto for organ and orchestra, 1954. Novello
48 Sinfonietta no. 1. 1954. Paterson
49 Ballet, *Rinaldo and Armida*, 1954. Faber
50 Serenade for guitar and strings, 1955. Paterson
51 Overture, *Tam O'Shanter*, 1955. Paterson
52 *John Clare* Cantata, f.p. 1955. Paterson
53 Little Suite no. 1 for orchestra, 1948. Paterson

54 Piano Trio, f.p. 1956. Paterson
55 Song of Praise, for unison voices and piano, pub. 1956. Paterson
56 Opera in one act, *The Open Window*, f.p. 1956. Unpublished
57 A Grand Grand Overture, 1956. Paterson
58 Concerto no. 2 for horn and strings, 1956. Paterson
59 Four Scottish Dances, for orchestra, 1957. Paterson
60 March, *HRH The Duke of Cambridge*, f.p. 1957. Paterson
61 Quartet for oboe and strings, 1957. Faber
62 Toy Symphony, 1957. Paterson
63 Symphony no. 3, f.p. 1957. Paterson
64 Commonwealth Christmas Overture, 1957. Unpublished
65 Sinfonietta no. 2, 1958. Paterson
66 Five William Blake Songs for contralto and strings, f.p. 1959. Studio Music
67 Concerto for guitar and chamber orchestra, f.p. 1959. Paterson
68 Ballet, *Sweeney Todd*, 1959. Faber
69 *Song of Simeon*, 1959. Faber
70 March, *Overseas*, f.p. 1960. Paterson
71 Symphony no. 4, 1960. Paterson
72 *Carnival of Animals*, f.p. 1960. Unpublished
73 Quintet for brass, 1961. Paterson
74 Symphony no. 5, 1960. Paterson
75 Divertimento no. 2 for orchestra, f.p. 1961. Paterson
76 *Grand Concerto Gastronomique*, for eater, waiter, food and orchestra, 1961. Unpublished
77 Concerto for two violins and string orchestra, 1962. Faber
78 Little Suite no. 2 for orchestra, 1962. Paterson
79 Ballet, *Electra*, 1963. Unpublished
80 Little Suite no. 1 for brass band, 1963. Paterson
81 Sinfonietta no. 3, 1964. Paterson
82 *Water Music*, for wind and percussion, f.p. 1964. Novello
83 *A Sunshine Overture*, f.p. 1964. Lost
84 Five Pieces for violin and piano, 1964. Paterson
85 Duo for two cellos, 1965. Novello
86 Fantasy for bassoon, f.p. 1966. Faber
87 Fantasy for clarinet, f.p. 1966. Faber
88 Fantasy for horn, f.p. 1966. Faber
89 Fantasy for flute, f.p. 1966. Faber
90 Fantasy for oboe, f.p. 1966. Faber
91 Four Cornish Dances, 1966. Faber
92 *The Turtle Drum*, children's play for television, f.p. 1967. Faber
93 Little Suite no. 2 for brass band, f.p. 1967. Henrees Music
94 March, *The Padstow Lifeboat*, f.p. 1967. Henrees Music

95 Symphony no. 6, 1967. Faber
96 *Trevelyan* Suite, for chamber ensemble, 1967. Faber
97 Overture, *Peterloo*, 1967. Faber
98 *Salute to Thomas Merritt*, for two brass bands and orchestra, 1967. Unpublished
99 *Anniversary* Overture, 1968. Faber
100 Fantasy for trumpet, pub. 1969. Faber
101 Fantasy for trombone, pub. 1969. Faber
102 Fantasy for tuba, pub. 1969. Faber
103 *The Song of Accounting Periods*, for voice and piano, f.p. 1969. Unpublished
104 Concerto for two pianos (three hands) and orchestra, 1969. Faber
105 Concerto for 28 players, 1970. Faber
106 Fantasy for audience and orchestra, f.p. 1970. Unpublished
107 Fantasy for guitar, f.p. 1971. Faber
108 Concerto for viola and chamber orchestra. 1971. Faber
109 *Song of Freedom*, for chorus and brass band, f.p. 1973. Henrees Music
110 Overture, *The Fair Field*, 1972. Faber
111 Concerto no. 2 for flute and orchestra, 1972. Faber
112 *A Flourish for Orchestra*, 1973. Faber
113 Symphony no. 7, 1973. Faber
114a Fantasy for brass band, f.p. 1974. Henrees Music
114b Two John Donne Songs, for tenor and piano, 1974. Roberton
115 Second Concerto for clarinet and orchestra, 1974. Faber
116 *Fantasy on a theme of John Field*, for piano and orchestra, 1975. Faber
117 Fantasy for harp, 1975. Faber
118 String Quartet no. 2, 1975. Faber
119 Cantata, *The Return of Odysseus*, 1976. Faber
120 Philharmonic Concerto, for orchestra, 1976. Faber
121 Sonata for flute and piano, 1977. Faber
122 Variations on a theme of Ruth Gipps, for orchestra, 1977. Faber
123 Symphony for Brass, 1978. Faber
124 Symphony no. 8, 1978. Faber
125 Concerto for trumpet and orchestra, 1982. Faber
126 Four Irish Dances, for orchestra, 1986. Faber
127 Fantasy for recorder, 1986. Faber
128 Symphony no. 9, 1986. Novello
129 Three Fantasies for piano. Unpublished
130 Fantasy for cello, f.p. 1987. Faber
131 Little Suite no. 3 for brass band, f.p. 1987. Studio Music

132 Brass Quintet no. 2, f.p. 1988. Faber
133 Concerto for recorder and chamber orchestra, f.p. 1988. Faber
134 Serenade for tenor and strings, *Contrasts*, 1988. Novello
135 Duo for two B flat clarinets. Unpublished
136 Shakespearean Cello Concerto, 1988. Novello
137 Divertimento for wind octet, 1988. Novello
138 Four Welsh Dances, for orchestra, 1989. Novello
139 *Flourish for a Battle*, for wind and brass, f.p. 1990. Novello
140 Fantasy for recorder and string quartet, 1990. Novello
141 *Robert Kett* Overture, f.p. 1990. Novello
142 *A Manx Suite* for orchestra, f.p. 1990. Novello

The Films of Malcolm Arnold

1947	*Avalanche Patrol* *Seven RAF Flashes*
1948	*Charting the Seas* *Two RAF Flashes* *Gates of Power* *Hydrography* *Report on Steel* *Badger's Green* *Mining Review* *Metropolitan Water Board* *Hawick, Queen of the Border* *Women in our Time* *Cotton – Lancashire's Time for Adventure*
1949	*EVWs* *This Farming Business* *Britannia Mews* *The Frazers of Cabot Cove* *Drums for a Holiday* *Terra Incognita* *The Beautiful County of Ayr* *Fight for a Fuller Life* *Trieste: Problem City* *Dollars and Sense* *Your Witness* *Julius Caesar* *Antony and Cleopatra*

	When You Went Away
	Science of the Orchestra
1950	*Oil Review No 5*
	ECA Productivity Team
	Fifty Acres
	Up for the Cup (composed by Percival Mackey, orchestrated by Arnold)
	Airways
	The Riddle of Japan
	Where Britain Stands
	This is Britain
	Let Go For'ard
1951	*Alien Orders*
	No Highway
	Home to Danger
	Power for All
	Men and Machines
	Wings of Danger
	Local Newspapers
	Home at Seven
1952	*Stolen Face*
	The Holly and the Ivy
	The Sound Barrier
	Channel Islands
	The Island
	Curtain Up
	The Ringer
	It Started in Paradise
	Four-Sided Triangle
	Invitation to the Dance
1953	*Gilbert and Sullivan* (arrangements by Arnold)
	The Captain's Paradise
	Man of Africa
	Copenhagen, City of Towers
	Albert RN
	You Know What Sailors Are
	Powered Flight: The Story of the Century
	Devil on Horseback
	Hobson's Choice

1954 *The Royal Tour – New Zealand*
The Sleeping Tiger
Welcome The Queen
Beautiful Stranger
The Belles of St Trinian's
The Sea Shall Not Have Them
The Constant Husband
A Prize of Gold

1955 *The Night my Number came up*
I am a Camera
Value for Money
The Deep Blue Sea
The Woman for Joe
1984

1956 *Port Afrique*
Trapeze
A Hill in Korea
Wicked as they Come
The Barretts of Wimpole Street (not used in the final version)
Tiger in the Smoke
The Rose Tattoo

1957 *Island in the Sun*
Blue Murder at St Trinian's
The Bridge on the River Kwai
Dunkirk

1958 *The Key*
The Roots of Heaven
The Inn of the Sixth Happiness
Coupe des Alpes

1959 *The Boy and the Bridge*
Solomon and Sheba (part only)
Suddenly Last Summer (in collaboration with Buxton Orr)

1960 *The Angry Silence*
Tunes of Glory
The Pure Hell of St Trinian's
No Love for Johnnie

1961	*Whistle Down the Wind* *On the Fiddle*
1962	*The Inspector* *The Lion* *Nine Hours to Rama*
1963	*Tamahine* *The Chalk Garden*
1964	*The Thin Red Line*
1966	*The Heroes of Telemark* *Sky West and Crooked* *The Great St Trinian's Train Robbery* *Africa – Texas Style*
1967	*North Sea Strike*
1969	*The Reckoning* *Battle of Britain* (composed by William Walton, expanded and partly scored by Arnold) *David Copperfield*

Select Bibliography

Writings by Malcolm Arnold

'I think of music in terms of sound', in *Music and Musicians*, July 1956, p. 9
'Finding the Money', in *Sunday Times*, 2 November 1958, p. 23
'Don't shoot the pianist', in the *Guardian*, 3 June 1971
'Music' (Malcolm Arnold writes about the music he enjoys), in the *Listener*, 14 October 1971, p. 518
'My Early Life', in *Music and Musicians*, October 1986, pp. 8–9

Interviews

with *The Times*, 14 May 1959
with Christopher Ford, in the *Guardian*, 17 April 1971
with Michael Oliver, *Music Weekly*, BBC Radio 3, January 1980
'Malcolm Arnold at 65', in *The British Bandsman*, 25 October 1986
with John Amis, *Music Now*, BBC World Service, 17 October 1986
'Malcolm Arnold – in harmony with Scotland', in *Dundee Courier and Advertiser*, 28 May 1987
with Piers Burton-Page, *Contrasts*, Central Television, 7 February 1989
with Peter Paul Nash, *Music Weekly*, BBC Radio 3, 14 October 1991
with Kriss Rusmanis, *Omnibus*, BBC Television, October 1991
with Margaret Howard, *Classic Reports*, Classic FM, 21 October 1992

Works Consulted

Adeney, Richard, *Flute*, unpublished memoir, 1987
Adler, Larry, *It Ain't Necessarily So*. London, Collins, 1984
Amis, John, *Amiscellany*. London, Faber & Faber, 1985
Arnold, William, 'Malcolm Arnold's Musical Ancestry', in *Musical Events*, November 1960, p. 8

Barker, Rachel, *Conscience, Government and War*. London, Routledge & Kegan Paul, 1982
Blades, James, *Percussion Instruments and their History*. London, Faber & Faber, 2nd edition, 1975
Blades, James, *Drum Roll*. London, Faber & Faber, 1977
Brymer, Jack, *In the Orchestra*. London, Hutchinson, 1987
Burton, Humphrey, *Leonard Bernstein*. London, Faber & Faber, 1994
Burton-Page, Piers, 'Malcolm Arnold and the String Quartet', in *The Musical Times*, October 1986, pp. 551–4
Burton-Page, Piers, 'Malcolm Arnold at 70', in *The Musical Times*, October 1991, pp. 493–5
Burton-Page, Piers, 'Arnold's Ninth', in *BBC Philharmonic Friends Magazine*, vol. 33, Winter 1991–2, pp. 8–10
Burton-Page, Piers, 'Six Paradoxes in Search of a Composer', in *From Silents to Satellite*, vol. 10, Autumn 1991, pp. 22–4
Cole, Hugo, 'Arnold's Fantasies', in *The Musical Times*, 1988, pp. 22–3
Cole, Hugo, *Malcolm Arnold – An Introduction to his Music*. London, Faber and Faber, 1989
Cole, Hugo, 'Malcolm Arnold at 60', in *Music and Musicians*, October 1981, pp. 9–11
Dunnett, Roderic, 'Malcolm Arnold: Freeman of Northampton', in *Musical Opinion*, March 1990, pp. 86–7
Evens, Tim, *Standing Up To Be Counted*. York, Ebor Press, 1988
Fawkes, Richard, 'Heights and Depths', in *Classical Music*, 19 October 1991
Fisher, Paul, 'Old Wild Child is back in tune', in *Sunday Telegraph*, 6 October 1991
Foreman, Lewis (ed.), *Edmund Rubbra – Composer*. Rickmansworth, Triad Press, 1977
Gradenwitz, Peter, *Leonard Bernstein – The Infinite Variety of a Musician*. Leamington Spa, Oswald Wolff Books, 1987
Greenfield, Edward, 'Norfolk Notes', in the *Guardian*, 7 July 1989
Hall, Patrick, *The Harp that Once*. London, Heinemann, 1967
Harries, Merion and Susie, *A Pilgrim Soul – The Life & Music of Elizabeth Lutyens*. London, Michael Joseph, 1989
Kallaway, William, *London Philharmonic*. Havant, Kenneth Mason, 1972
Kehoe, John, 'Malcolm Arnold', in *Conifer News*, no. 1, p. 1
Keller, Hans, *Criticism*. London, Faber & Faber, 1987
Keller, Hans, 'Malcolm Arnold's Third Symphony', in *Musical Events*, January 1958
Kennedy, Michael, *Portrait of Walton*. Oxford University Press, 1989
Lambert, Constant, *Music Ho! A Study of Music in Decline*. London, Faber & Faber, 3rd edition, 1966
McDonald, Donna, *The Odyssey of the Philip Jones Brass Ensemble*. Bulle (Switzerland), Editions BIM, 1990

Mason, Colin, *Music in London, 1951–1961*. London, Longmans Green, 1963
Mellor, David, 'What about Arnold?', in the *Spectator*, 7 December 1991, p. 41
Mitchell, Donald, 'Malcolm Arnold – An Introduction', in *The Musical Times*, August 1955, pp. 410–13
Mitchell, Donald, 'Malcolm Arnold and the Curse of Popularity', broadcast talk, BBC Radio 3, 14 March 1977
Mortimer, Harry, *On Brass. An Autobiography*. Sherborne, Alphabooks, 1981
Motion, Andrew, *The Lamberts*. London, Chatto & Windus, 1986
Palmer, Tony, *Julian Bream. A Life on the Road*. London, Macdonald, 1982
Peacock, Arthur, 'Arnold at 60', broadcast talk, BBC Radio 3, October 1981
Pettitt, Stephen J., *Dennis Brain. A Biography*. London, Robert Hale, 2nd edition, 1989
Pirie, Peter J., *The English Musical Renaissance*. London, Gollancz, 1979
Poulton, Alan, *The Music of Malcolm Arnold, A Catalogue*. London, Faber & Faber, 1986
Railton, Ruth, *Daring to Excel*. London, Secker & Warburg, 1992
Raynor, Henry, *Music in England*. London, Robert Hale, 1980
Ritchie, Christopher, 'Malcolm Arnold just writes what he would like to hear', in *Soundtrack*, pp. 5–9
Ritchie, Christopher, 'The Arnold–Lean trilogy', in *From Silents to Satellite*, vol. 10, Autumn 1991, pp. 26–32
Russell, Thomas, *Philharmonic Decade*. London, Hutchinson, 1944
Savage, Richard Temple, *A Voice from the Pit – Reminiscences of an Orchestral Musician*. Newton Abbot, David & Charles, 1988
Schafer, R. Murray, *British Composers in Interview*. London, Faber & Faber, 1963
Simpson, Robert, *The Proms and Natural Justice*. London, Toccata Press, 1981
Stasiak, Christopher, 'The Symphonies of Malcolm Arnold: Eclecticism and the Symphonic Conception', in *Tempo*, no. 161/2, June/September 1987, pp. 85–90
Tollington, Ruth, 'The Development of Malcolm Arnold's Musical Style, with Reference to Three of his Symphonies'. Unpublished dissertation, Cambridge College of Arts and Technology, 1988
Trend, Michael, *The Music Makers*. London, Weidenfeld & Nicolson, 1985
Vaughan, David, *Frederick Ashton and his ballets*. London, A. & C. Black, 1977
Woodcock, Sarah C., *The Sadler's Wells Royal Ballet*. London, Sinclair-Stevenson, 1991

Index